How to Jumpstart Your Medical Career and Thrive in Practice

Practical Advice and Insight from
a Battle-Tested Physician

∞

Arthur Lazarus, MD, MBA, CPE, DFAAPL

American Association for
PHYSICIAN
LEADERSHIP

Published by **American Association for Physician Leadership, Inc.**
PO Box 96503 | BMB 97493 | Washington, DC 20090-6503

Website: www.physicianleaders.org

13   8 7 6 5 4 3 2 1

Copyedited, typeset, indexed, and printed in the United States of America

PUBLISHER
Nancy Collins

PRODUCTION MANAGER
Jennifer Weiss

DESIGN & LAYOUT
Carter Publishing Studio

COPYEDITOR
Patricia George

ALSO BY ARTHUR LAZARUS

Neuroleptic Malignant Syndrome and
Related Conditions (co-author)

Controversies in Managed Mental Health Care

Career Pathways in Psychiatry: Transition in Changing Times

MD/MBA: Physicians on the New Frontier
of Medical Management

Every Story Counts: Exploring Contemporary Practice
Through Narrative Medicine

Medicine on Fire: A Narrative Travelogue

Narrative Medicine: The Fifth Vital Sign

Narrative Medicine: Harnessing the Power
of Storytelling through Essays

Story Treasures: Medical Essays and
Insights in the Narrative Tradition

21st Century Schizoid Health Care: Essays and Reflections
to Keep You Sane on Your Medical Travels

Narrative Rx: A Quick Guide to Narrative Medicine
for Students, Residents, and Attendings

Narrative Medicine: New and Selected Essays

Narrative Frontiers: Essays at the Edge
of Medicine and the Multiverse

Critical Condition: American Medicine
at the Quarter-Century Mark

Real Medicine, Unreal Stories: Lessons and Insights
from Clinical Practice

To all physicians at any stage of their journey —
may this book serve as a career guide
and path to discovery.

TABLE OF CONTENTS

AFTERWORD

"The greatest mistake you can make in life is to be continually fearing you will make one."

— ELBERT HUBBARD

About the Author

ARTHUR LAZARUS, MD, MBA, IS a healthcare consultant, certified physician executive, and nationally recognized author, speaker, and champion of physician leadership and wellness. He has broad experience in clinical practice and the health insurance industry, having led programs at Cigna and Humana. At Humana, Lazarus was vice president and corporate medical director of behavioral health operations in Louisville, Kentucky, and subsequently a population health medical director in the state of Florida.

Lazarus has also held leadership positions in several pharmaceutical companies, including Pfizer and AstraZeneca, conducting clinical trials and reviewing promotional material for medical accuracy and FDA compliance. He has published more than 450 articles and essays online and in scientific and professional journals. He has written and edited over a dozen books, including many related to the field of narrative medicine.

Born in Philadelphia, Pennsylvania, Lazarus attended Boston University, where he graduated with a bachelor's degree in psychology with distinction. He received his medical degree with honors from Temple University School of Medicine, followed by a psychiatric residency at Temple University Hospital, where he was chief resident.

After residency, Lazarus joined the faculty of Temple University School of Medicine, where he currently serves as an adjunct professor of psychiatry. He also holds non-faculty appointments as executive-in-residence at Temple University Fox School of Business and Management, where he received his MBA degree, and senior fellow, Jefferson College of Population Health, Philadelphia, Pennsylvania.

Well-known for his leadership and medical management skills, Lazarus is a sought-after presenter, mentor, teacher, and writer. He has shared his expertise and perspective at numerous local, national, and international meetings and seminars.

Lazarus is a past president of the American Association for Psychiatric Administration and Leadership, a former member of the board of directors of the American Association for Physician Leadership (AAPL), and a current member of the AAPL editorial review board. In 2010, the American Psychiatric Association honored Lazarus with the Administrative Psychiatry Award for his effectiveness as an administrator of major mental health programs and for expanding the body of knowledge of management science in mental health service delivery systems.

Lazarus is among a select group of physicians in the United States who have been inducted into both the Alpha Omega Alpha medical honor society and the Beta Gamma Sigma honor society of collegiate schools of business.

Lazarus enjoys walking, biking, playing piano, and listening to music. He has been happily married to his wife, Cheryl, for over 45 years. They are the proud parents of four adult children and the grandparents of six young children.

PREFACE

Welcome to *How to Jumpstart Your Medical Career and Thrive in Practice*. This book is a toolkit for physicians navigating the complex, often overwhelming realities of modern medicine. Whether you are just starting out, transitioning into a new role, or looking for ways to rekindle your passion for the profession, these essays offer practical insights, thought-provoking ideas, and a touch of inspiration to help you thrive.

Medicine is a field steeped in tradition but constantly evolving. The challenges we face as physicians today — from managing the administrative weight of practice to addressing burnout and maintaining meaningful connections with patients — require more than clinical expertise. They demand reflection, adaptability, and a willingness to embrace the human side of healthcare. In these pages, you will find discussions on the art of listening, the transformative power of storytelling, and the critical importance of professional accountability. You'll also encounter candid explorations of career pitfalls, strategies for personal growth, and the often-overlooked value of soft skills in advancing your career.

This book is written in an essay format and divided into two sections: *Practice* and *Career*. The first section focuses on the practice of medicine, emphasizing the nuances of patient care, communication, and the ethical dimensions of our work. Essays like "Taglines, Chief Complaints, and the Risk of Losing the Story" and "The Role of Physicians in Addressing Traumatic Invalidation" delve into the essential, often intangible aspects of our relationships with patients and colleagues.

The second section tackles the career aspects of medicine, offering practical advice on job interviews, leadership, and the hidden challenges of piloting your medical career. Pieces such as "Brutal Career Truths for Doctors (Read This Before It's Too Late)" and "A Physician's Guide to Recognizing Red Flags in Job Interviews" are grounded in real-world experience and designed to equip you with the tools to succeed.

The idea for this book arose from my own journey through medicine — one where practice eventually turned into a career in industry. During each phase — clinical and non-clinical — there were moments of triumph, doubt, and discovery, followed by reflections on lessons learned, stories shared, and observations made. I share them with you as both a mirror and a guide, helping you see your own path more clearly while offering actionable advice to overcome obstacles and seize opportunities.

As physicians, we are entrusted with the privilege and responsibility of healing. But to truly fulfill this role, we must also care for ourselves and our professional lives. This book is an invitation to step back, reflect, and recalibrate so that you can practice medicine with clarity, compassion, and purpose. Let these essays be your companion as you traverse the uncertain yet joyous terrain of this remarkable profession.

Thank you for allowing me to share this journey with you. May these pages inspire you to practice and live with intention, integrity, and a deep connection to the calling that brought you here.

PROLOGUE

∞

What Does It Mean to Be Battle-Tested?

*Career pathways are often decided by
how physicians deal with adversity.*

YOU MAY BE CURIOUS WHY I chose to subtitle this book *Practical Advice and Insight from a Battle-Tested Physician.* What makes me — or any physician, for that matter — "battle-tested"? The term implies more than just experience; it suggests someone who has been hardened by adversity, tested in the trenches, and emerged with hard-won wisdom. It describes a physician who has faced both the relentless demands of clinical medicine and the personal toll it exacts. That's where I come in.

Medicine is not just a profession — it's a crucible. Over the course of my career, I've been forged by the pressures of training, the emotional weight of patient care, and the ever-present challenge of balancing medical intuition with the constraints of a fragmented healthcare system. I've stood at the bedside of patients in their most vulnerable moments, navigated impossible ethical dilemmas, and witnessed firsthand the evolution — sometimes the decline — of healthcare as both an industry and an art. These experiences have shaped me into a physician who has, quite literally, seen it all.

But my career didn't end at the bedside. Like many in medicine, I reached a crossroads — one that led me to explore opportunities beyond traditional clinical practice. Moving into non-clinical roles was not a retreat but an evolution, allowing me to apply my expertise in new ways. Whether in leadership, consulting, or industry, I gained a broader perspective on the forces molding modern healthcare, from policy and economics to technology and innovation. In stepping beyond the hospital walls, I discovered that being a physician is about far more than direct patient care; it's about influence, adaptability, and using hard-earned wisdom to shape the future of medicine.

Now, as a battle-tested physician, I want to share what I've learned. This book is for medical students, residents, and attendings who seek more than just survival in medicine; they want to thrive. Whether you envision a lifelong clinical career or an eventual transition into new frontiers, my goal is to equip you with the insights, strategies, and unvarnished truths that only come from having walked the path myself.

Scars from the Battlefield

Of course, no one emerges from battle unscathed. The most searing wound of my career came early, when I was a first-year psychiatry resident on call. It was around midnight when a medical resident in the emergency department (ED) phoned me about a schizophrenic patient "hearing voices." She assured me that he was stable and only needed guidance on his antipsychotic dose. There was no need for me to see him in person. Relieved to avoid a late-night trek to the ED, I advised her on the medication and went back to bed.

At 3 a.m., the phone rang again. The same resident, now frantic.

"Dr. Lazarus, you're never going to believe what happened. That patient — we sent him to his boarding home, but the paramedics just brought him back. He jumped from a third-story window. Both legs are likely broken. He's in X-ray now — probably needs surgery. I just thought you should know."

I couldn't sleep after that. I replayed the conversation in my head, second-guessing myself — and her. The patient wasn't suicidal. He had no command hallucinations. He had been stable — or so I had been told. I should have gone to see him myself, I lamented. I should have known better.

By morning, the ED staff had already told the consultation–liaison team about the incident, and a rumor had spread that I had refused to see the patient. The shame set in like an IV infusion.

The house staff started calling him "the jumper." And me? I was the resident who let it happen.

I spiraled. Anxiety consumed me. I dreaded being on call. I shied away from difficult cases. Depression crept in, and my performance suffered — enough for my faculty to take notice. Though I eventually recovered with the help of a skilled psychiatrist, I never fully came to terms with what had happened. The weight of that night followed me throughout my career, lingering like an old wound that never quite heals.

I left clinical practice for industry roles in the pharmaceutical and health insurance sectors, where I faced a different kind of battlefield — one filled with bureaucratic obstacles, ethical gray zones, and the sobering realization that medicine, at its core, is not always driven by patient care alone. In these new arenas, I found challenges just as formidable as those in the hospital — different battles, but battles nonetheless.

For a time, I wondered if I was a *recovering* physician instead of a battle-tested one. I wrestled with my own identity. When I left clinical practice, people stopped addressing me as "doctor." I became just "Art." At dinner, wine helped take the edge off. During the COVID-19 pandemic, I abandoned wine for writing — a different kind of recovery, one that allowed me to process my experiences rather than numb them.

Why This Book Matters

So why am I telling you this? Because medicine is hard. Not just intellectually but emotionally, morally, and existentially. Every physician carries scars, whether they admit it or not. Some are fresh wounds, others long-healed but still tender to the touch.

This book is not just about how to build a career in medicine — it's about how to survive *and* thrive despite the battles you will inevitably face. It's about finding meaning, resilience, and maybe even joy in a profession that will test you at every turn.

The truth is, every physician who endures long enough becomes battle-tested. The question is: Will you emerge defeated, or will you emerge wiser?

I hope this book helps you claim the latter.

Section 1

PRACTICE

∞

Taglines, Chief Complaints, and the Risk of Losing the Story

*Deep dives into patients' histories often
reveal the true medical narrative.*

A FELLOW WRITER AND ARTIST and I were having an online exchange. She said her painting was being interrupted by bursts of writing. She texted, "I'm writing about how storytelling is liberating itself from commerce, politics, religion, and emerging as medicine and culture."

I asked if I could use her quote as my biographical tagline. On my LinkedIn profile, I could say: "I write about how storytelling liberates us from commerce, politics, and religion, emerging as medicine and culture."

"No," she replied. "That sentence is my life's journey rendered to clarity."

Oh well, so much for T.S. Eliot's advice, "good writers borrow, great writers steal." So, I came up with a tagline of my own: "Physician and author of stories that ignite passion, serving up medicine for the masses."

She called it "beautiful," and perhaps it is. But is it *me*? That's harder to say.

The Paradox of Taglines

Overall, I'm not too sanguine about the idea of letting a tagline define me, even though shorthand seems to be endemic in our culture. I think much of this trend has been brought on by social media and other fads, like fast dating. However, quick, unenthusiastic impressions may result in "false negatives." Taglines may turn off people who, if they took the time to dig a little deeper, would come to understand and appreciate you.

Taglines seduce us. They suggest clarity, confidence, and an invitation to be understood. Yet, in reducing ourselves to a handful of words, we risk being misunderstood — or worse, dismissed. The brevity that taglines demand plays into the societal shift toward quick judgments, one-liners, and snap impressions.

In a world dominated by social media, dating apps, and elevator pitches, people are increasingly defined by what they can project in seconds. This isn't inherently wrong — first impressions matter — but the cost is high. How many meaningful connections never form because someone is filtered out prematurely, their essence misjudged by an overly hasty evaluation?

For writers like me, taglines can be a kind of paradox. We understand the value of words and take pride in their ability to convey depth. And yet, a tagline demands we limit ourselves to a few pithy phrases that inevitably simplify who we are. It feels like an act of reduction, as though we must squeeze our complexities into a single, marketable moment.

The tension between depth and reduction feels strikingly familiar to me as a physician. Medicine, like taglines, often risks distilling people into categories: patient profiles, diagnoses, chief complaints, or even billing codes. In the hurried pace of clinical practice, it's easy to see a patient as "the diabetic in Room 3" or "the post-op knee replacement." These shorthand descriptors, while practical, obscure the richness of a person's story — the life they've lived, the challenges they face, the fears they carry.

The practice of medicine is ultimately the practice of presence, of seeing the whole person behind the label, just as we might hope others see the whole person behind a tagline. When we reduce patients to medical taglines, we lose not only the opportunity to connect deeply but also the chance to provide care that truly heals. A diagnosis is necessary, but it's not sufficient — it must be accompanied by an understanding of the individual it describes.

Taglines and medical shorthand both cater to assumptions and quick takes, creating missed opportunities for connection. Just as a tagline can leave others with a false impression of who we are, a clinical note or diagnosis code can do the same for a patient. Both fail to capture the fullness of the narrative, the depth that lies beneath. It's a reminder that true healing often requires a willingness to explore the layers of our own narratives rather than settling for simplistic or surface-level explanations.

Perhaps this is why I find taglines so unsatisfying. As a psychiatrist, I've spent years listening to patients' stories, digging deeper than what's immediately visible — and encouraging my patients to do the same. Peter Gabriel's song "Digging in the Dirt" is exactly about that: exploring the hidden layers of our psyche and confronting our fears and trauma. Gabriel explains it on his website (petergabriel.com) as discovering "some hurt that might later affect adult behavior." Patients' stories remind us that every person, every life, is more than a headline. The work of both medicine and storytelling is to resist easy reductions and to acknowledge the depth and complexity that make us human.

The Problem with the "Chief Complaint"

Does that mean taglines have no value? Not necessarily. They can be useful as starting points, hooks to draw people in. Perhaps that is why the "chief complaint" has persisted for millennia, and why I fell prey to its trappings as a busy first-year resident bouncing from chart to chart in the emergency department.

The chart I picked up had as the chief complaint: "sore on head." I pulled back the curtain of the exam room cubicle without bothering to read the history. I introduced myself, simultaneously scanning the young man's head. I didn't see a sore.

"Show me the sore," I said, drawing the curtain closed. He nonchalantly dropped his pants and pulled down his underwear to show me the sore on his "head."

"Oh, *that* head!" The situation called for penicillin, not a bandage.

We must resist the temptation to let our patients' complaints define them. They are more than a slogan or a sentence. They are more than their clinical signs and symptoms. Who they are unfolds over time, not in a single office visit.

Maybe the challenge isn't to abandon taglines altogether but to treat them with caution. They're tools, not truths — ways to open a door, not a final verdict. And for those willing to look beyond their patients' taglines, there's always more to discover.

The Physiological Power of Storytelling

Narratives transform listeners as well as readers of stories.

STORYTELLING IS AN ANCIENT HUMAN tradition, a bridge between generations that connects us through shared emotions and experiences. Scientific research highlights its powerful physiological and psychological effects, positioning it as more than a cultural practice.

Storytelling is also a potent therapeutic tool. Studies demonstrate that storytelling influences stress, pain, and emotional well-being, while additional research on the hormone oxytocin underscores the biological mechanisms that amplify these effects. Together, they illustrate storytelling's impact not only on listeners but also on storytellers.

The benefits of storytelling emerge clearly in pediatric healthcare settings, where it has been shown to reduce cortisol (a stress hormone) and pain perception while increasing oxytocin, which has been associated with bonding, empathy, and emotional resilience. One study examined storytelling's impact on children, comparing it to a non-narrative activity involving riddles. Through biomarkers like oxytocin and cortisol, alongside pain assessments and emotional expression analyses, the researchers uncovered compelling evidence of storytelling's benefits.[1]

Children who listened to stories experienced heightened oxytocin levels, reinforcing feelings of trust and social bonding. Simultaneously, cortisol levels dropped significantly. Beyond these physiological changes, storytelling influenced the emotions of young patients, resulting in positive associations with their caregivers and hospital environments. The transformation extended to language: children were exposed to stories that described nurses, doctors, and hospitals in kinder, more hopeful terms, reflecting an inner emotional recalibration.

The researchers attributed these outcomes to the immersive quality of narratives. Stories transport listeners to alternate realities, temporarily shielding them from distress while providing cognitive frameworks to process their experiences. This process, termed "narrative transportation," engages neural circuits associated with empathy, imagination, and social cognition. In the ICU setting, where fear, pain, and isolation dominate, storytelling becomes a lifeline, reconnecting children with their humanity and offering psychological relief amid adversity.

These findings align with broader research on oxytocin as a "natural medicine," which reveals its capacity to regulate stress responses, foster social connections, and even modulate immune functions.[2] Storytelling taps into this ancient biological system, offering listeners a temporary reprieve from their anxieties by transporting them to imaginative worlds where they can process emotions in a safe and constructive manner.

For children in intensive care units, storytelling provides a dual benefit: It reduces physiological stress markers and shifts emotional perceptions, promoting trust and facilitating positive connections with caregivers. Such findings suggest that the effects of storytelling are not merely cognitive but deeply embodied, mediated through neurochemical pathways that influence emotional states and physical health.

While much research focuses on storytelling's effects on listeners, the act of telling stories also provides substantial benefits for the storyteller. For adults, especially those reading to children or grandchildren, storytelling stimulates oxytocin release, strengthening bonds and enabling joining. Narrating stories encourages adults to revisit their imaginative capacities, cultivating a sense of wonder often lost in the rush of daily life. In grandparents, storytelling serves as a means of bridging generational divides, offering wisdom and comfort while reaffirming their role in the lives of younger family members.

The connection between storytelling and oxytocin further reinforces the idea that narratives are a biologically ingrained form of therapy. Oxytocin's anti-inflammatory and stress-modulating properties suggest that storytelling may have physical health benefits beyond its emotional impact. By increasing trust and emotional linkages, storytelling strengthens social bonds, which are themselves protective factors for health and well-being.

In an era increasingly defined by isolation and stress, the simple act of sharing a story offers a welcome antidote. It reminds us of our shared humanity, creating spaces where empathy, understanding, and healing can flourish. Whether soothing a child in a hospital bed or connecting with loved ones around a fire, storytelling embodies the interplay of science and humanism. It is an art form deeply rooted in our evolutionary history yet timeless in its relevance and power to heal.

Through storytelling, we honor one of our most enduring traditions while embracing its therapeutic potential. As science continues to uncover and elaborate the relationships between narrative, neurochemistry, and emotional health, storytelling remains a testament to the resilience and creativity of the human spirit — a force that connects, heals, and transforms, one story at a time.

REFERENCES

1. Brockington G, Moreira APG, Buso MS, *et al*. Storytelling Increases Oxytocin and Positive Emotions and Decreases Cortisol and Pain in Hospitalized Children. *PNAS*. 2021;118(22): e2018409118. https://doi.org/10.1073/pnas.2018409118
2. Carter CS, Kenkel WM, MacLean EL, Wilson SRE, *et al*. Is Oxytocin "Nature's Medicine"? *Pharmacol Rev*. 2020;72(4):829–861. https://doi.org/10.1124/pr.120.019398

Expanding Medical Writing Beyond Academia

*Always consider the ethical and professional
implications of your writing.*

In their article, "Microskills for Writing for Non-Academic Outlets," Adaira Landry and Resa E. Lewiss encourage physicians and academics to explore writing opportunities outside peer-reviewed journals.[1] They argue that writing for non-academic audiences can enhance public understanding of healthcare and establish the author as a thought leader. Benefits include quicker publication timelines, a broader audience, and potential professional growth through interdisciplinary collaborations.

They provide practical advice on topic selection, crafting unique angles, and pitching to appropriate outlets. Additionally, they stress the importance of authenticity, clarity, and tailoring content to different readerships.

Challenges with Traditional Publishing Models

Physicians increasingly turn to non-academic writing due to frustrations with traditional scientific publishing. Privately owned journals have faced significant criticism for prioritizing profits over science. Common complaints include rising publication fees, editorial mismanagement, and reduced support for essential processes like copy editing. For instance, the mass resignation of the editorial board of the *Journal of Human Evolution* highlights how profit-driven decisions, such as the decision to replace human oversight with AI, can degrade publication quality and trust.[2]

High fees also create barriers for researchers, particularly those from underfunded institutions or low-income regions. This exclusivity contradicts the principles of equality and inclusivity that many journals claim to uphold, prompting physicians to seek alternative avenues to share their insights.

The Ethical Landscape of Physician Writing

While the article by Landry and Lewiss is excellent for gaining an understanding of the technical and creative aspects of writing, it does not sufficiently address the ethical and professional dimensions involved in this pursuit. Physicians must consider how public writing interacts with their professional responsibilities and reputations. Physicians engaging in public discourse take on dual responsibilities — as writers and as medical professionals. This duality imposes a unique set of ethical and professional challenges that demand special attention.

Clarifying the Professional Identity of Authors

For example, physician-authors must explicitly define whether they write as independent practitioners, representatives of their institutions, or both. This distinction influences the tone, content, and potential implications of their work. A statement or opinion may carry more weight if perceived as institutional rather than personal. To avoid potential misunderstandings, writers should include disclosures clarifying their roles and affiliations.

Institutional Oversight and Compliance

Institutions often have policies governing public-facing communications by their employees, especially when the topics are controversial or sensitive. Consulting an institution's compliance office before submitting work for publication can help ensure alignment with organizational policies. Failure to do so may result in unintended breaches of confidentiality, intellectual property disputes, or reputational harm — both personal and institutional.

Ethical Risks in Narrative Storytelling

Storytelling is a powerful tool for engaging readers, but it also carries ethical risks. When physicians share personal experiences or clinical anecdotes, they must balance the need for compelling storytelling with the responsibility to maintain professionalism. Emotional narratives can sometimes lead to unintended consequences, including misinterpretation or ethical breaches.

Consent and Confidentiality in Clinical Vignettes

Publishing patient stories requires strict adherence to confidentiality. Even when identifying details are altered, the potential for recognition by patients or colleagues persists. Obtaining informed consent — preferably in writing — from the individuals involved is essential, including permission from family members featured in narratives.

Moreover, physicians should consider whether the story's educational or advocacy value outweighs the risks of exposure. When in doubt, seeking guidance from an ethics board or legal counsel can provide clarity.

Transparency and Conflicts of Interest

Many physician-authors write to promote ventures such as books, consulting services, or professional websites. While such pursuits are legitimate, they must be transparently disclosed to avoid undermining the credibility of the content. Readers should understand when a piece serves both educational and promotional purposes. Transparency builds trust and reinforces the physician's commitment to ethical practice.

Appeals of Autonomy and Broader Reach

Non-academic writing offers a level of autonomy and immediacy absent in traditional publishing. By bypassing bureaucratic processes and restrictive editorial practices, physicians can address timely issues directly. Platforms like blogs, op-eds, and independent publications empower them to shape public discourse without constraints imposed by academic standards.

Broadening Perspectives and Sharing Expertise

Writing for general audiences allows physicians to disseminate knowledge beyond the confines of academia. It can demystify complex medical topics, influence public health discourse, and highlight universal challenges. This engagement positions physicians as advocates for evidence-based medicine and compassionate care. However, public writing also exposes physicians to risks, including criticism, misrepresentation, or even legal challenges. Authors must prepare for these possibilities by ensuring their arguments are well-reasoned, supported by evidence, and free from sensationalism.

Building Thought Leadership
Physician-authors who write consistently and effectively for non-academic outlets often emerge as thought leaders in their fields. This role can lead to invitations for public speaking, consulting, or collaboration across disciplines. However, maintaining credibility requires an ongoing commitment to integrity and professionalism.

Conclusion

Writing for non-academic audiences offers physicians a valuable platform to share insights, educate the public, and advocate for change. By thoughtfully addressing ethical and professional considerations, physician-authors can maximize the impact of their work while preserving the trust and integrity essential to their role. Balancing storytelling, confidentiality, and transparency is critical to this process.

Physicians who embrace these challenges responsibly contribute not only to their personal growth but also to the broader advancement of medical knowledge and public understanding.

REFERENCES

1. Landry A, Lewiss RE. "Microskills" for Writing for Non-Academic Outlets. MedPage Today. January 17, 2025. https://www.medpagetoday.com/opinion/second-opinions/113828?trw=no.
2. Ouellette J. *Evolution* Journal Editors Resign en Masse. Ars Technica. December 30, 2024. https://arstechnica.com/science/2024/12/journal-editors-resign-to-protest-ai-use-high-fees-and-more/?comments-page=1#comments.

The Art of Listening in Medicine Is More Than a Skill. It's a Necessity

Adopting practices related to narrative medicine facilitates good listening.

I MET UP WITH A relative whom I had not seen in a long time. Our conversation turned to medicine.

"You don't need to be a genius to be a doctor," I told him. "You just need to know how to listen to your patients."

My relative, who is not a physician, added: "Patients need reassurance. They need friendly faces. They need receptionists who are actually receptive. They need angels of mercy. Furnishing these special features requires the sort of humility capable of appreciating that a healthcare system needs its patients as much as the patients need the system."

We agreed that in the fast-paced world of modern medicine, where technology and innovation drive much of the diagnostic process, doctors are losing the fundamental skill of listening to their patients.

Listening is the essence of effective clinical practice. Listening is more than just hearing words; it involves understanding the emotions, concerns, and contexts behind what a patient is saying. It's about creating a space where patients feel safe to express themselves fully, which can lead to more accurate diagnoses and better therapeutic outcomes. Here are some clinical examples that highlight the importance of listening in medicine:

1. **The Case of Unresolved Symptoms:** A 45-year-old woman presented with chronic headaches that had been resistant to various treatments. Multiple specialists had assessed her, focusing primarily on pharmacological interventions. During a consultation, a psychiatrist took the time to listen to her story

in detail, allowing her to describe her daily life, stressors, and emotional state. It was through this empathetic listening that the psychiatrist discovered her headaches were linked to severe anxiety stemming from unresolved grief. By addressing the underlying emotional issue, the patient experienced significant relief from her symptoms.

2. **The Misdiagnosed Condition:** A young man was diagnosed with irritable bowel syndrome (IBS) after presenting with gastrointestinal distress. However, his symptoms persisted despite treatment. A physician who practiced active listening noticed the patient often mentioned his symptoms worsened with certain life events. Through careful listening and questioning, the physician uncovered that the patient had a history of celiac disease in his family, which had been overlooked. Subsequent testing confirmed the diagnosis, and with dietary changes, his symptoms improved dramatically.

3. **Building Trust with a Reluctant Patient:** A teenage patient with diabetes was frequently missing appointments and not adhering to her treatment plan. Instead of reprimanding her, her physician decided to listen attentively to her reasons. The patient revealed her fear of needles and a feeling of alienation from her peers due to her condition. By listening, the physician was able to address her fears, arrange for alternative insulin delivery systems, and connect her with a support group. This approach helped improve her compliance and overall health.

4. **Addressing Cultural Sensitivities:** In a multicultural society, understanding a patient's cultural background can significantly affect care. An elderly patient from a non-Western culture was experiencing unexplained weight loss and fatigue. By listening to the patient and her family, the physician learned about her dietary habits and cultural practices. This understanding led to a culturally sensitive care plan that respected her traditions while addressing her nutritional needs, resulting in improved health.

Listening is an indispensable tool in a physician's repertoire. It creates trust, uncovers hidden diagnoses, and leads to more personalized and effective patient care. As technology evolves, the human touch provided through attentive listening remains irreplaceable. By mastering this art, physicians can ensure they not only treat diseases but also heal patients in the truest sense.

Mastering the Art

To master the art of listening, physicians must cultivate a set of deliberate practices that prioritize patient-centered communication. This begins with creating a welcoming environment where patients feel comfortable sharing their concerns. In the case of my relative, this did not happen.

He said that in order to make eye contact with his physician, he had to turn his neck 45 degrees. When the doctor tapped on their computer, computerized notes were helpfully projected onto a screen on the wall — but viewing them required him to turn his neck 90 degrees.

When he mentioned this complication to his doctor, the physician invited him to move to a less comfortable (and also immobile) bench in the corner, where he could view the doctor (albeit from a greater distance) without turning his head but could not view the screen on the wall without craning his neck by 180 degrees! "I was beginning to feel like Linda Blair, doing her full 360 in *The Exorcist*," he said.

Once patients are comfortable in the exam room and physicians feel unencumbered by technology, they should practice active listening techniques, such as maintaining eye contact, nodding affirmatively, and minimizing interruptions. This signals to the patient that their words are valued. Reflective listening, where the physician paraphrases or clarifies what the patient has said, can also be beneficial, ensuring understanding and allowing patients to expand on their thoughts.

Additionally, physicians should be mindful of their body language and tone of voice, as these nonverbal cues significantly affect patient perception. By being fully present and attentive, physicians can pick up on subtle emotional cues and underlying issues that might otherwise be missed. Regularly seeking feedback from patients and engaging in self-reflection can help physicians continually refine their listening skills.

The Practice of Narrative Medicine

I recommend that physicians take up the practice of narrative medicine, which enhances empathic listening by encouraging them to view patients' stories as central to the healing process. This approach emphasizes the importance of understanding the narrative context of a patient's life, which includes their personal, familial, and cultural backgrounds. By engaging with patients' stories, physicians can develop a deeper empathy and appreciation for their experiences.

Narrative medicine training often involves exercises in writing and reading, which help physicians process their own experiences and biases and generate a more open and empathetic mindset. This practice not only aids in understanding the patient's perspective but also helps build stronger therapeutic relationships, as patients feel heard and understood on a more personal level. Ultimately, narrative medicine bridges the gap between clinical expertise and compassionate care, enriching the doctor-patient interaction through shared stories and mutual understanding.

While recounting his story, my relative reminded me that his doctor's visit occurred in a new state-of-the-art building resembling a modern Eiffel Tower. "Surely it doesn't cost $762 million to teach employees to listen?" he asked incredulously.

Patients Suffer When Doctors Use Biased and Inflammatory Language

Biased language adversely affects the quality of care and worsens health disparities.

PRACTICING PSYCHIATRY MY ENTIRE CAREER, I can't begin to tell you how many "difficult" and "problem" patients I treated, many of them "addicted," "drug seeking," and "homeless." This is a true statement, deliberately worded unprofessionally.

Language is one of the most powerful tools in healthcare, shaping perceptions, attitudes, and outcomes. When biased or inflammatory language infiltrates medical discourse — whether in patient records, professional conversations, or discussions with patients — it can perpetuate stereotypes, damage trust, and negatively affect patient care. Such language, often subtle and unintentional, reflects deeper systemic biases that undermine the principles of equity and compassion foundational to medical practice.

Biased and Inflammatory Language in Medical Records

Bias in medical records refers to the phenomenon whereby healthcare providers use stigmatizing language in patient notes, often expressing negative attitudes toward patients, which can be based on factors like race, social class, or perceived patient behavior, potentially affecting the quality of care patients receive and contributing to health inequities.

Studies have found that physicians often use language in medical records that questions patient credibility, expresses disapproval of patient choices, stereotypes patients based on race or social class, portrays them as argumentative or problematic, and emphasizes physician authority over the patient. Black patients are more likely to have stigmatizing language in their medical records compared to White patients. The same is true of homeless patients. Biased language can negatively influence how other healthcare providers perceive and treat the patient, potentially leading to disparities in care quality and diagnostic errors.[1]

Specific Examples of Biased and Inflammatory Language

One common instance of biased language is the use of descriptors like "non-compliant" or "difficult patient." These labels reduce a person's complex circumstances to a pejorative term, disregarding potential barriers such as financial hardship, mental health struggles, or lack of understanding about their condition or treatment.

For example, a patient labeled "non-compliant" for missing appointments might actually lack transportation or childcare. Instead of uncovering and addressing these barriers, such language predisposes healthcare providers to blame the patient, fostering judgment rather than empathy.

Inflammatory language is also prevalent in discussions of substance use. Referring to someone as a "drug abuser" or "addict" stigmatizes their condition and frames their illness as a moral failing rather than a medical issue. This can lead to delayed or inadequate treatment, as healthcare providers may unconsciously deprioritize or approach such patients with bias. A more neutral, person-first alternative, such as "a patient with substance use disorder," shifts the focus to the medical condition rather than the person's character.

Coded racial or gendered language also appears in clinical settings. For instance, Black patients are more likely to be described as "agitated" or "angry" in medical notes, while White patients exhibiting similar behaviors are often characterized as "concerned" or "anxious." Women, particularly those presenting with pain, are frequently dismissed as "emotional" or "dramatic," leading to delays in diagnosis and treatment. A landmark study revealed that women with acute cardiac symptoms were less likely than men to receive appropriate diagnostic testing or intervention, in part because their symptoms were trivialized.[2]

Another study involved recording medical and pediatric residents doing "handoffs," and it found that biased phrases were more common in notes about patients who were Black or obese.[3] The biased handoffs were one of three types: stereotype, blame, or doubt.

An example of a biased handoff with blame concerned an adult patient with diabetes who "cut her dose in half 2 months ago because she was having some falls and thought she was getting hypoglycemic but never actually checked her blood glucose." The neutral version of that handoff was rephrased to describe someone who "cut her dose in half after experiencing hypoglycemic symptoms."

A follow-up study found that residents and medical students recalled clinical information with less accuracy after hearing a patient handoff rife with biased language. In addition, these young physicians had less positive attitudes toward patients after hearing biased handoffs.[4]

Outcomes of Biased and Inflammatory Language

The repercussions of such language are extensive. For patients, it can erode trust, diminish the quality of their care, and exacerbate health disparities. For example, a patient whose concerns are dismissed as "hysterical" may hesitate to seek medical care in the future, worsening their condition. Similarly, perpetuating stigmatizing language around mental health or addiction can discourage patients from disclosing symptoms or pursuing treatment, entrenching cycles of illness and inequity.

Biased language also affects healthcare teams. As implied from these research studies, a resident who reads a chart describing a patient as "difficult" might enter the room primed to have a negative interaction, missing cues that could lead to a more productive conversation. This ripple effect can alter how the entire team approaches the patient, reinforcing patterns of dismissiveness and substandard care.

Changing the Narrative

To reverse the harms of biased and inflammatory language, clinicians must cultivate self-awareness and adopt practices that emphasize objectivity and compassion. Using person-first language, avoiding subjective labels, and explicitly noting barriers to care rather than ascribing blame are small but powerful steps. For example, instead of "homeless," a clinician might write, "The patient is experiencing housing instability" or "The patient is currently without permanent housing." These phrases are more descriptive and less likely to carry negative connotations.

Physicians are not saints. They have biases and stereotypes like everyone else. If clinicians can accept that they're human and acknowledge their prejudices, they can try to reduce the impact of implicit and other biases on the care of patients — that level of honesty and introspection goes a long way.

Bias training, reflective writing, and mentorship can also play critical roles in shifting the culture of medical language. By framing patients' stories in ways that honor their dignity and humanity, we align more closely with the principles of patient-centered care and narrative medicine.

Ultimately, recognizing the power of our words is not just an ethical obligation but a clinical imperative, because how we speak about our patients shapes how we care for them. Conversely, stigmatizing language decreases our investment in the patient's well-being and hinders the development of a therapeutic relationship by creating barriers to trust and open communication.

REFERENCES

1. Brooks KC, Raffel KE, Chia D, Karwa A, Hubbard CC, Auerback AD, Ranji SR. Stigmatizing Language, Patient Demographics, and Errors in the Diagnostic Process. *JAMA Intern Med.* 2024;184(6):704–706. doi:10.1001/jamainternmed.2024.0705

2. Arber S, McKinlay J, Adams A, Marceau L, Link C, O'Donnell A. Patient Characteristics and Inequalities in Doctors' Diagnostic and Management Strategies Related to CHD: A Video-Simulation Experiment. *Soc Sci Med;* 2006;62(1):103–115. https://doi.org/10.1016/j.socscimed.2005.05.028

3. Wesevich A, Patel-Nguyen S, Fridman I, *et al.* Patient Factors Associated with Biased Language in Nightly Resident Verbal Handoff. *JAMA Pediatr.* 2023;177(10):1098–1100. doi:10.1001/jamapediatrics.2023.2581

4. Wesevich A, Langan E, Fridman I, *et al.* Biased Language in Simulated Handoffs and Clinical Recall and Attitudes *JAMA Netw Open.* 2024;7(12):e2450172. doi:10.1001/jamanetworkopen.2024.50172

The Fantasy of Reliving the Past Provides Lessons for Personal Growth and Patient Care

*We can't go back in time, but we can learn from
our mistakes and make course corrections.*

A TRANSPORTER MALFUNCTION CHANGES CAPTAIN Picard and several crew members into 12-year-old children in the Star Trek: The Next Generation episode "Rascals," which first aired on October 30, 1992. They retain their adult memories and intelligence, which enables them to fend off a revolt by Ferengi (a nemesis species) who hijack the Enterprise. Picard and the others are eventually restored to their normal status as adults (although one member chooses to delay the process).

Before it is known whether the affected crew can be transfigured back into adults, Counselor Deanna Troi attempts to comfort a pre-adolescent Captain Picard and prepare him for the possibility that he must grow up again. Picard is not pleased with the idea, feeling as though his life would be moving backward instead of forward. Heck, what I wouldn't give to relive the past, at least parts of it! What about you?

The Fantasy of a Redo

The fantasy of reliving your past — a "redo" — is perhaps one of the most intriguing and universally appealing concepts. Many people are drawn to the opportunity to revisit pivotal moments in their lives with the wisdom and experiences they've since acquired. This notion taps into the human desire for self-improvement and the wish to correct past mistakes or make different choices that could lead to a more fulfilling present.

Fantasizing about redoing certain things in our lives offers valuable insights into what we truly value and how past experiences have shaped the individuals we are today. In a broader sense, the concept of a "redo" invites us to consider how we can apply lessons from our past to our current lives without actual time travel. It encourages mindfulness and the active pursuit of growth and change, allowing us to shape a better future by learning from what has come before.

Doing something over by reliving the past with newfound wisdom is particularly relevant in the field of medicine, both in terms of medical practice and patient experiences. In medicine, learning from past experiences is crucial for continual improvement and better patient outcomes.

For physicians, the idea of a redo can be seen in the commitment to lifelong learning and the practice of reflective medicine. Doctors regularly review and analyze previous cases, outcomes, and treatment approaches to enhance their skills and knowledge. This reflective practice is akin to reliving past experiences with the aim of identifying what worked well and what could be improved. By doing so, physicians refine their techniques, adopt new technologies, and integrate the latest research findings into their practice, thereby moving the field of medicine forward.

Patients often wish for a redo when reflecting on past health decisions or actions. One common scenario involves delayed medical attention. Many patients regret not seeking care sooner when symptoms first appeared, particularly in cases where early intervention could have led to a better prognosis, such as with cancer diagnoses or heart disease.

Lifestyle choices also frequently prompt a desire for a redo. Patients often wish they had made healthier decisions in the past, such as adopting a better diet, exercising regularly, or avoiding smoking and excessive alcohol consumption. These regrets highlight the long-term impact of lifestyle on overall health.

Another scenario involves non-adherence to treatment plans. Patients sometimes regret not following their prescribed treatments, whether it involves taking medications as directed, attending follow-up appointments, or engaging in recommended physical therapy.

Such non-adherence can lead to worsened conditions or preventable complications.

Elective procedures can also lead to regret, especially if outcomes were not as expected or if complications arise. Patients may wish they had made different choices regarding surgeries or other elective interventions.

Issues around informed consent and decision-making are also common sources of regret. Patients sometimes wish they had sought more information or a second opinion before making a significant health decision, particularly in complex cases where multiple treatment options exist and the best course of action is not clear-cut, such as whether to have joint replacement or back (spinal) surgery, as opposed to opting for conservative treatment options.

Finally, some patients reflect on their mental health and stress management, wishing they had sought help earlier for mental health issues or developed more effective coping strategies to manage stress. Recognizing the effect of mental health on physical well-being often comes in hindsight.

Moving Forward

Whether the fantasy of a redo is expressed by a physician or a patient makes little difference. The essence is not about dwelling on past mistakes but rather about using those experiences as a foundation for improvement and growth. It emphasizes the importance of learning and adaptation, ensuring that healthcare providers and patients can move forward with greater insight and preparedness for future challenges.

Captain Picard believed that the thought of moving backward rather than forward felt like a loss of progress and identity, especially given his accomplishments and responsibilities as captain of the Enterprise. He was not persuaded by Counselor Troi's suggestion that he could obtain another degree at Starfleet Academy or take a sabbatical and study geology or archaeology, should he not be able to return to his adult status and be forced to relive his past.

As physicians, we could easily understand why Picard might feel this way. Would you want to repeat college, medical school, or residency, even with advanced knowledge of the subject matter? The thought of repeating those experiences can be daunting and undesirable, including reliving past traumas and attempting to correct them.

While the notion of a redo might offer theoretical opportunities, the practical and emotional realities make it an unattractive option for me. Perhaps I would have asked for help more often or tried to improve bad relationships. I certainly wouldn't have obsessed as much on my mistakes and shortcomings, and I would have learned to worry less about my patients by not making their problems mine.

If We Could Turn Back Time

Still, the $64,000 question is: Would I choose to become a doctor at all?

Here is how family medicine physician Tomi Mitchell, MD, answered the question: "[I]f I could go back in time [w]ould I say, 'Run for the hills — it's a dumpster fire!' or caution that not all that glitters are gold? Would I still choose this path? The truth is, I absolutely would. Yes, there are challenges — moral injuries, broken systems, and days that stretch far too long. But the heart of medicine, the privilege of being there for people during their most vulnerable moments, still shines."[1]

I feel the same way, too — with one caveat: the only "redo" I'm inclined to take now, in my eighth decade, is a mulligan for a bad putt in my mini-golf game.

REFERENCE

1. Mitchell T. If I Could Talk to My Younger Self Before Medical School." KevinMD.com. February 4, 2025. https://kevinmd.com/2025/02/if-i-could-talk-to-my-younger-self-before-medical-school.html

Certification, Licensure, and Professional Accountability

The importance of balancing free speech, ethics, and patient trust.

BOARD CERTIFICATION IS A MARKER of expertise and adherence to evidence-based practices within a specialty. It signifies that a physician has met rigorous standards and remains committed to upholding them. When an organization like the American Board of Internal Medicine (ABIM) revokes certification, it's not merely a symbolic act; it's a signal to the public and the medical community that the individual has failed to meet these standards.

The ABIM's revocation of a prominent physician's board certifications has reignited debates about free speech, medical ethics, and professional accountability.[1] The doctor, once a respected cardiologist, became a polarizing figure during the COVID-19 pandemic due to controversial claims about treatments and vaccines. The repercussions of these statements — and the ABIM's subsequent actions — raise questions about the boundaries of professional responsibility and the consequences of spreading misinformation in a public health crisis.

In this case, the doctor's promotion of unproven treatments such as hydroxychloroquine and outspoken criticism of COVID-19 vaccines — including claims that tens of thousands of Americans died from vaccination — were at odds with prevailing medical evidence.

Physicians wield significant influence, and their words carry weight, especially during a crisis. Misinformation from a credentialed expert can undermine public trust, fuel conspiracy theories, and jeopardize lives. The ABIM's decision underscores its responsibility to safeguard the integrity of the profession and protect patients from harm.

Free Speech versus Professional Responsibility

Critics of the ABIM's decision argue that it infringes on physicians' free speech rights. They suggest that the ABIM could face legal challenges for penalizing opinions, particularly in a climate where guidance by government agencies has become ambiguous after purging medical content from their websites.

On the other hand, while the First Amendment protects individuals from government censorship, it does not shield professionals from actions taken by professional organizations for the consequences of disseminating harmful or misleading information in their capacity as experts. Physicians, by virtue of their training and ethical obligations, are expected to prioritize evidence-based care and avoid causing undue harm.

Many applaud the ABIM's actions as a necessary measure against "snake oil sales" and "witch doctor" practices. A prevailing sentiment is that doctors who make up medical advice in the middle of a deadly pandemic based on politics instead of science deserve to have their credentials revoked. This perspective emphasizes the ethical obligation of physicians to adhere to rigorous scientific standards, particularly when public health is at stake. Trust in the medical profession depends on its members acting as stewards of reliable, evidence-based information.

Medical Licensure Implications

While board certification is an important credential, medical licensure granted by state medical boards ultimately determines whether a physician can practice medicine. State medical licensing boards have the authority to investigate complaints, impose disciplinary actions, and revoke medical licenses if physicians are found to violate professional standards. These boards operate independently of certification bodies like the ABIM and are tasked with protecting public health and safety.

In this case, the physician's medical license remains active in two states, highlighting a potential gap between certification revocation and licensure status. State medical boards may face pressure to act when a physician's actions bring widespread scrutiny, particularly if those actions are deemed harmful to the public. Consistency and coordination between licensing boards and certifying bodies are essential to maintaining public trust in the medical profession.

However, a lack of coordination among state medical boards and the absence of a centralized licensing authority can create challenges in addressing problematic behavior uniformly. Physicians who face disciplinary actions in one state may still retain licensure in others, enabling them to continue practicing despite significant concerns about their conduct.

A more integrated approach — such as a national database or standardized reporting system — could enhance transparency and ensure that disciplinary actions are applied consistently across state lines. Such reforms would strengthen the accountability mechanisms that protect patients and uphold professional standards.

Implications for the Medical Community

The ABIM's decision raises broader questions for the medical community: How should professional organizations address dissenting voices within their ranks? Is there a threshold where contrarian views become harmful enough to warrant disciplinary action? In balancing free speech with professional responsibility, it is essential to distinguish legitimate scientific debate from the propagation of falsehoods that endanger public health.

Moreover, this case highlights the need for clear guidelines on professional conduct during public health crises. Consistency in enforcement can help maintain public trust and reinforce the principle that professional freedom comes with the responsibility to uphold ethical and evidence-based standards.

Conclusion

The revocation of the physician's board certifications is a clear reminder of the professional responsibility of being a doctor during a public health emergency. While debate will persist about the boundaries of free speech and medical accountability, the primary focus must remain on protecting patients and preserving the integrity of the medical profession. The actions of the ABIM signal a commitment to these principles, serving as a cautionary tale for physicians who stray from evidence-based practices in favor of personal or political agendas.

REFERENCE

1. Fiore K. ABIM Revokes Certification of Another Doctor Who Made Controversial COVID Claims. *J Med.* January 15, 2025. https://www.namd.org/journal-of-medicine/3353-abim-revokes-certification-of-another-doctor-who-made-controversial-covid-claims.html

What I Do as a Physician

Exploring the interplay of mentorship, reflection,
and the evolution of medical practice.

IN DONALD FAGEN'S 2006 SONG "What I Do," the singer-songwriter imagines a conversation between his younger self and the ghost of Ray Charles. The interplay of generations, guidance, and self-discovery within the song's narrative provides a poignant lens through which to examine the life of a physician — a profession that is, in many ways, a perpetual dialogue between the past, present, and future.

Fagen seems to grow from his fictitious encounter with Charles, learning that finding his "bad self" was the key to his success. For doctors, the question of "What I Do" also involves a search for authenticity and purpose. Their job extends beyond technical aspects to encompass an internal conversation with the ideals that drew them to medicine, the wisdom imparted by their mentors, and the personal experiences that shape their practice.

Medicine begins, for many, as an act of aspiration, often influenced by personal health experiences. Like Fagen's younger self, seeking insight, young physicians-in-training look to their mentors for guidance, hoping to bridge the gap between their idealism and the vagaries of real-world practice. This guidance often comes not as direct instruction but as stories, reflections, and the subtle modeling of behaviors (my cherished mentor had a beard; I grew one too). The attending who shares a tale of failure — and the lessons learned from it — or the seasoned clinician who pauses to comfort a grieving family, reminds the young doctor of the central human connection at the heart of "what they do."

My mentors, primarily psychiatrists, demonstrated their expertise both at the bedside and behind one-way mirrors — and with remarkable clarity and no "smoke-and-mirrors." They specialized in treating patients with severe depression and psychosis, practicing with a confidence and conviction that they conveyed to even the most hesitant residents. For instance, my co-resident, who was caring for a highly suicidal patient who had miraculously survived an oncoming train, was initially reluctant to "push" the patient into therapy. Our supervisor advised, "The difference between you and me is that you're afraid of that damn train, and I'm not."

As the years and trains roll on, the dialogue turns inward. The young doctor transforms into that striking, seasoned physician, their professional life shaped by the cumulative weight of decisions, triumphs, and regrets. The once-vivid ideals may fade, challenged by the grind of administrative tasks, the constraints of a broken healthcare system, or the emotional toll of caring for the sick and dying.

In such moments, the song's reflective tone offers a kind of solace: the recognition that the search for meaning is ongoing, that "what I do" is rooted in identity as much as in action. As the lyrics suggest, "It's in my DNA. It's what I do." This duality of practice and essence captures the heart of medicine's journey.

The ghost of a physician's younger self is never far away. It appears in the form of eager and wide-eyed medical students who ask probing questions that remind their mentors of the ideals they once held dear. It emerges in the quiet moments of reflection after a long day, when a particular patient's story lingers in the mind, prompting a reevaluation of priorities and values. And it speaks in the lessons taught to others, the stories shared, and the legacy built through acts of care and mentorship.

Patients, too, are part of this ongoing dialogue. Each interaction is a microcosm of "What I Do," a chance to reaffirm the purpose of medicine. The ghost of Ray Charles, in Fagen's song, offers not definitive answers but a presence — a witness to the younger self's struggles and growth. Similarly, patients offer physicians a reflection of their own humanity. Their resilience, vulnerability, and courage remind doctors of the higher calling that drew them to the profession and challenge them to rise above the noise of bureaucracy and routine.

What Do I Do?

Ultimately, "What I Do" is a song about the search for meaning, and it is this search that defines the life of a physician and reaffirms them. The answers are never final; they are formed by experience, relationships, and the rapidly changing landscape of medicine. Physicians carry with them the voices of their mentors, the echoes of their younger selves, and the stories of their patients. In these voices, they find not only guidance but also the enduring question that sustains them: "What do I do?"

What do I do when the test results arrive too late, and a patient's condition has already worsened? What do I do when a family looks to me for hope I cannot provide? What do I do when an exhausted resident falters, and I must decide whether to push or protect them? What do I do when a colleague makes a mistake, and I must weigh loyalty against accountability? What do I do when, late at night, I question whether the sacrifices I've made were worth the cost?

These questions are not anomalies; they are the quiet undercurrent of a physician's life. Answers are often elusive, and perhaps that is the point. It is in the asking, in the struggle to reconcile these moments, that the essence of "What I do" takes shape.

The beauty of "What I do" — and asking the question "What do I do?" — lies in its openness. It allows for growth, reflection, and adaptation. It acknowledges that medicine is not merely a profession but a journey — a conversation between who we are, who we were, and who we aspire to become. Just as Fagen's dialogue with Ray Charles weaves together the past and present, the work of a physician is a continuous interplay of memory, practice, and prospect. "What I do" is not just a statement; it is a story unfolding one patient, one moment, one lesson at a time.

The Boy and The Koi

Reflections on stillness, medicine, and legacy.

THE PHOTO CAPTURES A YOUNG BOY standing at the edge of a koi pond, his small figure framed by the lush surrounding greenery. The pond's surface shimmers with sunlight, casting dappled reflections of the trees above. Beneath the surface, koi of every hue — brilliant oranges, whites, and golds — glide gracefully through the clear water. The boy leans slightly forward, his gaze intent, as though the fish hold the secrets of the universe. Around him, the world hums with life, yet he is still, captivated by the serene dance of the koi.

The boy at the koi pond stands on the edge of a quiet moment, his gaze fixed on the rippling water as vibrant shapes glide beneath the surface. The world around him, bustling with activity, fades into the background. In this scene, there is an undeniable purity — a rare suspension of time. The koi swim in practiced arcs, their scales shimmering with light, reflecting not just the sun but a tranquility that seems almost otherworldly. This moment, suspended and serene, holds a lesson for medicine.

Physicians, much like the koi in their deliberate movement, are trained to navigate complex, sometimes dangerous, waters. Yet the beauty of their work often lies in the moments of stillness — the quiet pauses when they step back to consider not just the data but the humanity within their care. The boy's unbroken gaze reminds us of the importance of attention untainted by distraction, of engaging fully with the present. For patients and practitioners alike, this act of reflection can transform the clinical encounter, allowing room for clarity and connection.

The koi themselves are a symbol of resilience, adaptability, and grace. They are a mirror for the patient's journey through illness. Like the koi's unhurried swim, healing often demands patience and a willingness to let the currents guide the way. Patients, too, benefit from moments of stillness — pauses in the constant stream of appointments, treatments, and tests — to gather their strength, find perspective, and recalibrate their hopes. The pond becomes a metaphorical space where transformation feels possible.

For many physicians, the boy's curiosity is a reminder of why they entered the field. Before the pressures of efficiency and metrics, there was awe — a desire to understand the wonders of medicine and its vast secrets. Over time, medical practice can dull this initial spark, burying it beneath layers of routine and responsibility. Yet moments like the one at the koi pond offer a chance to reclaim that curiosity. A quiet reflection on the arcs of a patient's story, much like the koi's arcs through water, can reinvigorate a sense of purpose.

Even the pond itself holds meaning. Its surface, reflecting both sky and child, conceals a world beneath — complex, alive, and constantly moving. This duality mirrors the practice of medicine. The surface shows the charts, symptoms, and protocols, while underneath lie the intricate narratives of human experience, the unspoken truths submerged beneath the surface: the resilience of the human spirit, the depth of patient stories, and the shared vulnerabilities that connect us all. To penetrate the surface requires intentional focus, a willingness to pause and ponder what is unseen but deeply felt.

What adds a layer of wonder to this image is knowing its origin. The setting is a college campus, a place of learning and innovation. My son, a creative writing instructor there, captured the photo. The boy in the frame is his 3-year-old son. This connection imbues the scene with a profound sense of legacy, reminding me that the lessons we draw from the moment are not merely for medicine but for life itself. Just as a college campus fosters growth and reflection, the pond and its koi become symbols of the deep and ongoing process of learning.

The boy and the koi remind us that stillness and reflection are not luxuries; they are essential. For physicians, they provide the space to think, adapt, and rediscover purpose. For patients, they offer a reprieve, a chance to gather strength and see beyond the immediacy of illness. And for medicine as a whole, they serve as a gentle call to return to what matters most: the shared humanity in the moments that connect us.

In the stillness of the pond, the arcs of the koi, and the quiet gaze of the boy, I see not just a fleeting moment but the enduring power of reflection and connection passed through generations. This image resonates deeply, linking my work in narrative medicine to the broader currents of creativity and care that ripple through our lives. It is a legacy not only of writing and storytelling but of attentiveness — a reminder to pause, observe, and engage with the world's quiet beauty and its eloquent truths hidden beneath the pond's surface.

Connection: The Gift That Keeps on Giving

Gratitude is the spark that lights a connection — and the wonder of awe sustains it.

MEDICINE, AT ITS CORE, IS a human endeavor, and in medicine, connections are more than relationships; they are lifelines. From the first hesitant interaction between physician and patient to the deeply rooted bonds forged over years of care, these connections define the practice of healing.

Connection is the gift that keeps on giving, enriching not only the patient but the healer as well. The doctor-patient relationship is the cornerstone of effective healthcare, fostering trust, empathy, and understanding. The act of connecting with patients goes beyond diagnosing and treating ailments; it involves listening to their stories, understanding their fears, and acknowledging their humanity. Such a connection offers psychological comfort that can significantly enhance clinical outcomes.

Studies have shown that patients who feel understood and supported are more likely to adhere to treatment and report higher satisfaction with their care.[1] Furthermore, connection extends beyond individual interactions to encompass the broader healthcare community. Collaborative teamwork among healthcare professionals enhances patient care and creates an environment where knowledge and expertise are shared. This interconnectedness is a gift that continuously enriches the practice of medicine, driving innovation and improving patient outcomes.

Gratitude as the Spark

Gratitude is the spark that illuminates these connections. A patient's simple "thank you" can pierce through the numbing exhaustion of a 12-hour shift. Conversely, a physician's gratitude for the privilege of being entrusted with another's health can reframe a routine day into a meaningful journey.

Today's hurried pace overlooks the power of gratitude in the healthcare setting, especially for physicians. Cultivating gratitude can lead to greater job satisfaction, enhanced resilience, and feelings that overshadow burnout. Acknowledging the privilege of caring for patients can reinvigorate a physician's sense of purpose.

For patients, expressing gratitude can improve their mental well-being and lead to a positive outlook on their health journey. Gratitude encourages patients to focus on the support and care they receive, reinforcing their connection with healthcare providers and strengthening their resolve to overcome health challenges. This reciprocal exchange of gratitude between patient and physician creates a positive feedback loop, enriching the healthcare experience for all involved.

I once cared for a poor elderly woman who brought me little, inexpensive gifts every so often, such as a pair of socks. Any gift was beyond her means, and as a psychiatrist, I understood that receiving gifts from patients had ethical implications. However, I recognized that these offerings were not about material value. They were tokens of her gratitude — gestures that carried emotional significance.

To her, these small gifts were a way to convey a deep appreciation for being seen and heard in a world where she often felt demeaned. Accepting them with sensitivity and care allowed me to honor the connection we had built and the trust she placed in me. It reminded me that gratitude, when given so earnestly, is a two-way street. Her gifts became a symbol of our relationship — an unspoken acknowledgment of the bond we had formed and the healing space we shared.

Similarly, expressing gratitude to my mentors and colleagues deepened my connection to the profession itself. A simple note of thanks to a mentor for their guidance or a word of appreciation to a colleague for their advice became more than just gestures of politeness. These acts reinforced the shared purpose and mutual respect that underpin the practice of medicine.

Gratitude fostered a sense of camaraderie and reminded me that, in a field often marked by isolation and stress, we are stronger together. Acknowledging the contributions of those around me not only respected their efforts but also rekindled my own passion for the work, creating a ripple effect of encouragement and renewal.

The Wonder of Awe

While gratitude ignites connection, awe sustains it. Moments of awe in medicine often arrive unexpectedly: witnessing the first breath of a newborn, marveling at the determination of a patient who defies grim odds, or simply observing the intricate choreography of a beating heart.

Awe is humbling. It reminds physicians of the vast mysteries that remain unsolved and underscores physicians' role as stewards of both knowledge and compassion. In an era dominated by algorithms and efficiency, awe re-centers us on the beauty of human life. More than that, awe has an element of vastness that makes us feel small; this tends to decrease our mental chatter and worries and helps us think about ideas, issues, and people outside of ourselves, improving creativity and collaboration.

For example, during my first year of residency, a young woman was admitted to the psychiatry unit in the throes of severe psychosis. Initial doses of antipsychotic medication had no effect. Her labs came back two days later, revealing thyrotoxicosis (too much thyroid hormone). Following the definitive treatment — a subtotal thyroidectomy — I visited the patient, now in the surgical wing of the hospital. Her mental status had returned to normal. I watched the family embrace her, and I felt an overwhelming sense of awe. It wasn't just the surgery that brought her back; it was the collective effort of a connected team, buoyed by hope and guided by care.

Sustaining the Human Spirit

While gratitude and awe together create a self-sustaining loop, energizing physicians and patients alike, maintaining this loop requires intentional effort in an increasingly fragmented healthcare system. Physicians must carve out time for reflection, finding moments to appreciate their role in life's most sacred events. Patients can nurture these connections by recognizing their physicians as partners in care rather than mere "providers" of service.

The challenge lies in resisting cynicism — a creeping erosion of connection that threatens the very soul of medicine. Burnout, administrative burdens, and the dehumanization of care can extinguish both gratitude and awe. Yet, even amid these challenges, I believe the essence of medicine endures. The gift of connection, once kindled, has the power to regenerate itself, lighting the way forward.

Conclusion

It's been said many times that medicine is not just a science; it is an art. Connection is perhaps the least appreciated aspect of the art of medicine. Gratitude fuels it, awe sustains it, and together, they form the foundation of a practice that heals both body and spirit. In every clinic, hospital, and hospice, these elements quietly shape lives. They remind us why we chose this path and renew our commitment to walking it, one patient, one connection, at a time.

REFERENCE

1. Krist AH, Tong ST, Aycock RA, and Longo DR. Engaging Patients in Decision-making and Behavior Change to Promote Prevention. *Stud Health Technol Inform*. 2017;240:284–302.

ESSAY 12

The Role of Physicians in Addressing Traumatic Invalidation

The virtue of healing patients by validating
their emotions and experiences.

TRAUMATIC INVALIDATION OCCURS WHEN AN individual's experiences, emotions, or perceptions are dismissed, minimized, or denied in a way that causes them deep psychological harm. Understanding this concept is critical for physicians, as invalidation can occur both inadvertently and as a direct result of practice. Recognizing and addressing invalidation is essential to establishing trust, empathy, and effective communication with patients and colleagues.

Recognizing Invalidation in Clinical Encounters

In clinical encounters, invalidation often stems from time pressures, implicit biases, or a focus on biomedical explanations over psychosocial factors. For instance, dismissing a patient's symptoms with phrases like "it's all in your head" or "it's just stress" can leave patients feeling unheard and disrespected.

Such interactions also undermine the therapeutic relationship and contribute to patient harm, as individuals may delay seeking care or lose confidence in the healthcare system. The experience of being treated as "dependent" or having pain dismissed with an overdose kit instead of validation illustrates the damaging effects of such invalidation.

Invalidation often begins in childhood. A patient frequently dismissed with phrases like "Stop crying, it's not a big deal" may internalize the belief that their emotions are unworthy of attention. These early patterns can shape lifelong behaviors, leading to difficulties in expressing or trusting emotions. Physicians who recognize

43

these patterns can use empathy and validation to help patients rebuild emotional trust and resilience.

Understanding Trauma's Subjective Nature

Trauma is not defined solely by what happens but by how an individual is affected by the event. The same experience may affect people differently based on their unique histories, vulnerabilities, and coping mechanisms. For some, invalidation may compound existing trauma, while others may not experience it as acutely.

To support healing, both the trauma of what happened and the trauma wounds stemming from unmet needs must be addressed. Physicians should remain attuned to these instances to provide personalized care.

Supporting Individuals in Denial or Reluctant to Seek Help

Some individuals who experience lifelong invalidation may struggle to acknowledge their needs or seek help. Physicians can play a key role in gently guiding such patients toward support. This involves creating a safe environment, practicing patient-centered communication, and acknowledging the individual's experiences without judgment. Encouraging small, manageable steps toward professional help and validating their courage in doing so can bring about trust and openness.

Invalidation Within Healthcare Teams

Invalidation may manifest within healthcare teams as dismissive or undermining behaviors among colleagues. A resident might hear, "You're overreacting," when expressing concerns, or a nurse's observations might be dismissed as irrelevant. Such behaviors erode team morale and can jeopardize patient safety. Physicians, particularly in leadership roles, have a responsibility to model and promote a culture of respect and validation, ensuring that all voices are heard and valued.

Systemic Invalidation and Its Impacts

On a systemic level, invalidation often targets marginalized groups. Patients from underserved communities may encounter practitioners who dismiss their experiences of discrimination or fail to recognize the role of social determinants of health. Similarly, institutional policies prioritizing efficiency over individualized care can dehumanize patients and providers. Physicians must advocate for systemic changes that promote equity and validate the diverse experiences of patients and colleagues.

Psychological Consequences of Invalidation

The psychological toll of invalidation can be significant, eroding a person's ability to trust their own feelings and perceptions. This often leads to difficulties in identifying, processing, and expressing emotions. Chronic invalidation may contribute to internalized self-doubt, emotional numbness, or symptoms of PTSD. For individuals with pre-existing trauma, invalidation can amplify their suffering, leading to hypervigilance or dissociation.

Strategies for Physicians to Mitigate Invalidation

Physicians can mitigate the impact of invalidation by cultivating empathy and practicing active listening. Simple affirmations like "That sounds really challenging" or "I'm here to help you through this" can validate a patient's experience and build trust. Additionally, building a supportive and respectful environment within healthcare teams is essential for promoting psychological safety and collaboration.

Maintaining Professional Boundaries and Self-Awareness

Physicians must remain mindful of their own biases and blind spots that may lead to invalidating behaviors. Reflective practices, such as mindfulness or peer discussions, can help maintain empathy and prevent burnout. Encouraging open dialogue among team members about concerns and ideas reinforces a culture of mutual respect and accountability.

Supporting Patients Who Have Experienced Invalidation

For patients with histories of invalidation, referrals to mental health professionals, support groups, or advocacy networks can be life-changing. Physicians should educate patients about the interconnectedness of mental and physical health, emphasizing the validity of their emotions and experiences. Empowering patients to take an active role in their care helps promote healing.

Conclusion

Traumatic invalidation leaves deep scars, but physicians have the power to orchestrate healing and recovery. Physicians can strengthen therapeutic alliances and promote patient-centered care by validating emotions, addressing systemic inequities, and creating safe, empathetic spaces. Recognizing invalidation as a source of harm is crucial in advancing compassion and effectiveness in healthcare.

A Health Executive's Harrowing Experience as a Patient

An insider's journey through cancer care.

I READ ABOUT A HEALTHCARE executive who faced the life-altering reality of becoming a cancer patient. Many people share first-person accounts on the internet, but when healthcare professionals encounter impersonal and upsetting interactions as patients, they sometimes are motivated to write about those experiences — experiences that illuminate sad truths about the state of modern healthcare.

This patient's journey was particularly striking because of the initial inhumanity and unsettling initiation into the treatment process despite seeking care at a nationally recognized hospital.

The first surgeon offered a grim prognosis in a five-minute consultation, dismissing surgical options without discussion of goals or context. The second physician, a radiation oncologist, provided a conflicting recommendation in an equally brief encounter, suggesting surgery over radiation but warning against undergoing surgery at that institution. Neither physician sought to understand the patient's medical knowledge, personal aspirations, or fears. The cumulative effect of these encounters was a deep sense of isolation and mistrust compounded by the radiation oncologist's vote of no confidence in their own institution.

After six — yes, six! — second opinions, the journey led the physician to the world-renowned Memorial Sloan Kettering Cancer Center, where care transformed into collaboration. Here, a surgeon and a radiation oncologist reviewed the patient's history together before their first meeting. Their approach was rooted in empathy, teamwork, and respect for patient autonomy. They explored treatment goals, shared their expertise, and developed a plan that aligned with the patient's preferences. This experience underscored a critical truth: Trust and understanding are the foundation of world-class healthcare.

Reflecting on the journey, the healthcare executive identified many issues undermining patient care today. Productivity-based compensation models incentivize efficiency over empathy, while the corporatization of medicine treats physicians as interchangeable laborers, eroding morale. When physicians feel unappreciated and overburdened, patients may bear the brunt of their frustration.

To counter these trends, the executive proposed two pivotal changes. First, healthcare institutions must acknowledge the intrinsic connection between physician well-being and patient care. Salary-based compensation models, like those at Memorial Sloan Kettering, enable doctors to devote the time and attention each patient deserves. Moreover, creating a culture of emotional engagement across all levels of staff ensures patients feel supported and valued.

Second, organizations must leverage and respect the leadership skills of their physicians. Empowering physicians with substantial control over their practices and integrating them into governance structures can enhance engagement, reduce burnout, and improve outcomes. Institutions that adopt this model not only achieve financial stability but also enable physicians and patients to thrive.

Call to Action

Beyond the thoughtful changes proposed by the healthcare executive, transforming healthcare to prioritize empathy and excellence demands a broader overhaul. First, medical education should be restructured to embed communication skills, empathy, and cultural competence as core competencies. There is no reason empathy should wane as early as the third year of medical school, as studies have shown.

Training programs should emphasize the humanistic side of medicine, ensuring that future physicians learn how to engage meaningfully with patients. Including narrative medicine in the curriculum can help doctors appreciate the importance of patients' stories, teaching them to see beyond symptoms and diagnoses.

Second, healthcare systems must adopt technology in ways that enhance, rather than hinder, the doctor–patient relationship. Electronic health records (EHRs) are frequently cited as sources of burnout due to their time-intensive nature. Streamlining EHR systems to reduce administrative burden while preserving essential data-sharing capabilities can free physicians to focus on patient care. Incorporating AI tools for routine tasks, like scribing or diagnostic support, can further alleviate cognitive overload, allowing physicians to engage more deeply with their patients.

Third, healthcare institutions should prioritize workplace well-being through policies that address burnout and promote mental health. Structured mentorship programs, peer support groups, and confidential counseling services can create an environment where physicians feel valued and supported. Offering flexible schedules, adequate time off, and manageable patient loads ensures that doctors can maintain their passion for medicine without compromising their health.

Finally, patients must be empowered to participate actively in their care. Healthcare systems should openly share information about treatment options, risks, and outcomes. When shared decision-making is the norm, conversations tend to respect patients' values and goals. Creating feedback loops where patients can rate and review their experiences — not simply their doctor — can also help institutions identify and address gaps in care (see essay 22).

These changes, coupled with the executive's recommendations, can redefine healthcare as a partnership rooted in trust, compassion, and mutual respect. By prioritizing both physician well-being and patient empowerment, the system can evolve to deliver care that is not only effective but also deeply humane.

The fact that the problems were exposed by a healthcare executive lays bare another undeniable truth: healing must begin within the system itself. Physicians who are cared for and valued can extend that care and value to their patients. A patient's journey from despair to optimism — marked by a shift from impersonal to compassionate care — serves as a testament to the potential for transformation in healthcare.

As the executive now looks forward, post-surgery and optimistic about the future, their story carries a vital message. To achieve world-class care for patients, we must first ensure world-class support for those who provide it. Experiences like this remind us that we can build a system where empathy and excellence are the norm, not the exception.

Behind the Mask of the Mental Health Caregiver

Reflections on the mental health of
mental health professionals.

IMAGINE STANDING IN A ROOM filled with mental health profession-als: therapists, counselors, psychologists, psychiatrists. Now consider this: Half of the people in that room may be struggling with burnout, a quarter might be quietly battling depression, and others may be silently grappling with feelings of hopelessness.

These are the individuals we rely on to hold our pain, yet they often bear their own burdens in isolation. The irony is as heart-breaking as it is real: Those who help us heal often struggle to find healing for themselves.

The Weight of the Profession

Mental health professionals dedicate their lives to others, listening to trauma, unraveling pain, and creating safe spaces. But they are not immune to the weight of their work. Research paints a sobering picture: Burnout affects 50–70% of mental health professionals. Symptoms of depression are reported by 25-30% of psychologists. Alarmingly, the suicide risk for mental health practitioners is higher than in the general population.[1]

These numbers aren't just statistics — they're stories of real peo-ple who carry the emotional weight of others without a lifeline for their own struggles. Jokes about the field often stop abruptly when someone's loved one needs help. Suddenly, the undervaluation and underappreciation of these professionals become glaringly apparent.

The Silence That Hurts

Why is it so hard for mental health practitioners to say, "I need help"? The answers are layered, like the complexities of human emotions they untangle every day. Stigma, even within their field, perpetuates the fear of being labeled as "weak" or "unfit to practice." A culture of self-sacrifice teaches practitioners to prioritize clients over their own needs.

Many workplaces fail to provide adequate support systems for those on the frontlines of mental healthcare. Additionally, there is a persistent societal myth that they should "have it all together" and be immune to depression as, say, a cardiologist should be immune to heart disease. What nonsense!

The Cost of Isolation

When mental health professionals succumb to their struggles, the ripples can be seen and heard. Patients lose a trusted guide, colleagues lose a peer, and families are left to navigate unimaginable grief. The 2019 death by suicide of Gregory Eells, the executive director of counseling and psychological services at the University of Pennsylvania, underscores this stark reality.

Eells, a respected expert on resilience, jumped to his death from the 17th floor of a building in Philadelphia. Just six months into his role, Eells found himself overwhelmed by the demands of the job, compounded by the distance from his wife and three children, who were still living in Ithaca, New York.

Eells' mother shared with *The Philadelphia Inquirer* that he had been down in recent months, describing the position as more challenging than he anticipated.[2] Despite encouragement from his family to step away, he remained committed until his struggles overtook him.

His death not only shattered those who knew him but also left pressing questions about the huge gaps in support for professionals tasked with safeguarding the mental health of others — in this case, troubled college students. His story is a tragic reminder of the immense pressure these roles carry and the dire consequences when support systems fail.

Eells' passing also echoes a broader crisis at the University of Pennsylvania, which has experienced at least 14 student suicides since 2013.[2] This institutional history highlights the urgent need for structural change within mental health services to prioritize the well-being of both clinicians and those they serve. The silence around these tragedies is deafening, and the cost of ignoring the mental health of caregivers is far too high.

The Permission to Be Human

It's time to rewrite the story. Mental health practitioners are not superheroes — they're human. Vulnerable. Brave. Beautifully imperfect. By acknowledging their humanity, we take the first step toward building a healthier, more compassionate mental health system.

Mental health professionals should feel empowered to speak out and open up to trusted colleagues or friends. They need to set boundaries, learn to say no (see essay 20), step away, and protect their energy.

Seeking therapy, even as a therapist, provides a neutral space to unload and process their struggles. When I was a psychiatric resident, personal psychotherapy was expected. Staying connected and leaning into professional communities fosters greater self-awareness and can help reduce feelings of isolation and stress.

Building a Culture of Compassion

This isn't just a practitioner's issue — it's a collective one. When those who care for us are supported, the entire community benefits. We must destigmatize vulnerability within the profession and society at large. Advocating for better workplace support systems and mental health infrastructure is crucial. Encouraging early conversations about self-care and expert support during training can lay a foundation for resilience and well-being.

The road ahead is challenging but not impassable. It begins with recognizing that mental health professionals deserve the same care and compassion they extend to others. Just as they teach us that healing starts with acknowledging the wound, we must start by acknowledging their needs. Together, we can break the silence, honor their humanity, and ensure that those who guide us through the darkest moments have their own light to follow. Let's care for those who care because they deserve it, too.

REFERENCES

1. Sherry S. Why Are Psychologists at Greater Risk of Suicide? *Psychology Today*. June 26, 2024. https://www.psychologytoday.com/us/blog/psymon-says/202302/why-are-psychologists-at-greater-risk-of-suicide
2. Snyder S. Penn's Head of Counseling and Psychological Services Dies by Suicide at Center City Building. *Philadelphia Inquirer*. September 9, 2019. https://www.inquirer.com/news/university-of-pennsylvania-death-psychological-services-20190909.html

Bearing the Weight of Trauma and Finding the Path to Healing

Doctors are continuously exposed to trauma
— both direct and indirect effects.

TRAUMA IS PERVASIVE IN THE lives of physicians, and it emerges early in training. A study involving 1,134 interns revealed that 56.4% reported experiencing trauma during their internship.[1] Yet trauma often remains unacknowledged or misunderstood. The emotional toll of witnessing suffering, dealing with unexpected patient outcomes, and enduring practice pressures accumulates over time, leaving many doctors vulnerable to physical and mental health challenges.

Understanding Trauma in Medical Practice

Trauma encompasses deeply distressing or disturbing experiences, including direct physical harm, witnessing suffering, or feeling powerless. For doctors, trauma arises in various forms, such as acute trauma from sudden, critical incidents like patient deaths or medical errors. Chronic trauma results from repeated exposure to suffering, grief, and high-pressure environments. Studies suggest that between 15–30% of residents experience symptoms of post-traumatic stress disorder (PTSD), often linked to repeated exposure to patient distress and loss of life.

Most of this trauma is considered "vicarious" or "secondary." Nevertheless, physicians often carry the emotional residue of hearing patients' painful stories or witnessing their experiences. Despite these realities, medical training tends to emphasize resilience but rarely prepares individuals for the emotional impact of medical practice. Compounding this issue, the healthcare system's culture of stoicism discourages vulnerability and creates barriers to seeking help.

Trauma by Specialty

Not all specialties are created equal when it comes to exposure to trauma. Each specialty brings unique challenges, resulting in differential rates of PTSD, with emergency medicine, trauma surgery, pediatrics, psychiatry, and critical care ranking among the highest.

For emergency physicians, chaos is the baseline. Resuscitating a child who has drowned or informing parents of a teenager's fatal car accident are examples of the acute and relentless trauma they face. The pace of emergency medicine leaves little room for processing emotions, as another ambulance is always pulling in, presenting yet another life to save — or lose.

Trauma surgeons, by contrast, walk a tightrope between precision and exhaustion. Their trauma often stems from the visual and procedural aspects of their work, such as dealing with crash victims and repairing gunshot wounds. Additionally, the emotional echoes of surgical cases linger long after the surgeries conclude. The sterile field they work within can also become an emotional barrier, as they compartmentalize grief to maintain the steady hands their patients depend upon.

Pediatricians face a distinct form of anguish: witnessing a child's prolonged suffering or delivering terminal diagnoses to families. The natural optimism many bring into the field is often eroded by the devastation they encounter, leaving them grappling with a profound sense of helplessness.

Psychiatrists, though focused on the mind, are not immune to trauma. They bear the heavy burden of knowing that some patients might harm themselves despite their best efforts. The stories of their patients' past traumas can lead to secondary PTSD, adding another layer of emotional weight. Furthermore, the prevalence of aggression and violence from patients, coupled with the reality that many have patients who die by suicide, compounds the emotional toll.

In critical care, the intensity of trauma is amplified in the high-stakes environment of intensive care units. Physicians must balance medical expertise with emotional engagement as they manage cases involving multi-organ failure or prolonged life-support withdrawal.

The constant confrontation with life-and-death decisions often leaves deep scars on those who work in these settings.

Effects of Trauma on Physicians

The impact of trauma on physicians affects the emotional, physical, and professional aspects of life. Mentally, trauma increases susceptibility to anxiety, depression, burnout, and PTSD. Physicians often experience flashbacks, hypervigilance, and lingering feelings of guilt. Physically, chronic stress from trauma can manifest as sleep disturbances, hypertension, and other stress-related illnesses.

Professionally, unaddressed trauma can impair decision-making, reduce empathy, and lead to detachment from work, ultimately affecting the quality of patient care. Unfortunately, the stigma surrounding mental health in the medical profession exacerbates these challenges, often leaving physicians isolated and struggling silently.

Coping and Long-Term Strategies

When trauma strikes, treatment should not be delayed. Processing the critical event(s) is important because, if untreated, symptoms of PTSD may emerge months — even years — later. In the short term, grounding techniques, such as focusing on present realities or engaging in sensory experiences, can help doctors regain their composure. Support networks, whether through trusted colleagues, mentors, or mental health professionals, provide a space to process experiences. Journaling can also serve as a reflective practice to understand emotions and find clarity.

Sustained healing may require ongoing efforts by mental health professionals. Therapeutic interventions, such as cognitive behavioral therapy (CBT), eye movement desensitization and reprocessing (EMDR), pharmacotherapy, and arts-based therapies, can help physicians process and move past their experiences. Peer support groups offer a vital sense of community, reducing isolation and providing valuable coping strategies. Additional measures, such as mindfulness training, workplace wellness programs, and education on trauma resilience, can further mitigate the effects of trauma. These programs should be incorporated into medical schools and residency programs to help future physicians recognize and address trauma while breaking the stigma surrounding mental healthcare.

Overcoming Barriers

Seeking help for trauma is often hindered by fear of professional repercussions or being perceived as weak. Many physicians lack access to resources or knowledge about trauma-informed care, making it even more challenging to address their struggles. To overcome these barriers, healthcare systems must adopt trauma-informed principles. This approach includes creating safe spaces where physicians feel comfortable sharing their experiences, offering confidential counseling services, and advocating for policy changes that prioritize mental health. These efforts not only help physicians but also strengthen the medical profession by ensuring doctors can continue to provide high-quality care.

Conclusion

Physicians dedicate their lives to caring for others, often at the expense of their own well-being. Acknowledging and addressing the trauma inherent in their work is vital to sustaining the profession and improving patient care. By embracing a culture of support and resilience, the medical community can empower physicians to heal and thrive while continuing to serve others.

REFERENCE

1. Vance MC, Mash HBH, Ursano RJ, *et al*. Exposure to Workplace Trauma and Posttraumatic Stress Disorder Among Intern Physicians. *JAMA Netw Open*. 2021;4(6):e2112837. doi:10.1001/jamanetworkopen.2021.12837

Coaching by Doctors for Doctors

Doctors guided by professional physician coaches usually emerge healthier and happier practitioners.

THE DEMANDS OF MODERN MEDICINE are relentless. Physicians across the spectrum, from medical students to seasoned attendings, face escalating pressures from administrative overload to the emotional toll of patient care. Addressing these challenges requires targeted, evidence-based interventions designed by those who truly understand the unique struggles of the profession. This is where coaching by doctors for doctors becomes a vital lifeline.

The Power of Physician Coaching

A host of literature underscores the effectiveness of physician coaching in combating emotional exhaustion, impostor syndrome, stress, and burnout. Beyond reducing these pervasive challenges, coaching fosters resilience, self-compassion, and a greater sense of well-being.

Emerging evidence continues to highlight the major impact of coaching programs tailored specifically for overburdened physicians and doctors-in-training. Doctor-led coaching offers an unparalleled depth of understanding. Physicians who have "walked the corridors" and "worn the scrubs" bring unique insights and empathy to their coaching relationships. These MD and DO coaches have faced the challenges of medicine and emerged stronger, equipped to guide others along the same path.

A Lifespan Approach to Coaching

Coaching programs for physicians are designed to address needs across all stages of a medical career. Medical students benefit from support in developing a growth mindset, navigating critical feedback, and managing the transition into clinical practice. Residents gain tools to manage impostor syndrome, perfectionism, and the grueling demands of postgraduate training.

Attendings and medical leaders receive guidance in setting boundaries, structuring work-life balance, and building healthy relationships while addressing the unique pressures of leadership roles. Pre-retirement physicians explore ways to find meaning and navigate the emotional aftermath of stepping away from practice.

Coaching provides a safe, doctor-only space, free from the oversight of employers or training institutions, to tackle these challenges head-on. These confidential environments allow physicians to speak openly about their struggles without fear of judgment or professional repercussions. Physicians who receive coaching are considered clients, not patients, and there is no formation of a doctor-patient relationship or duty to disclose.

Transformational Topics

Physician coaching focuses on areas often neglected in traditional medical education and training. Programs may include cognitive and positive psychology techniques to reframe challenges, strategies for managing bullying, harassment, and litigation stress, and tools to promote mental health awareness and reduce suicide risk.

Coaching also addresses practices for maintaining work-life balance and developing healthy relationships. These interventions not only address immediate concerns but also cultivate long-term resilience and career satisfaction.

The Role of Peer-Support Groups

Alongside one-on-one coaching, anonymous peer-support groups provide another crucial resource. These confidential spaces — often virtual — foster connections among healthcare practitioners who share similar struggles. Participants engage in candid, stigma-free discussions, supported by peers who understand their pain without needing to know their names. The ethos of these groups, summarized in the mantra "No name, no shame," creates a safe haven for physicians to share their burdens.

Regular participation in peer-support groups reduces isolation, builds relationships, and models positive coping behaviors. Over time, these groups develop into cohesive, self-sustaining communities that provide enduring support through shared challenges.

The Immediate Implications of Burnout

While coaching is a powerful tool, it does not address all the issues underlying physician burnout. These challenges include overwhelming workloads, chaotic work environments, administrative burdens, and declining autonomy. The transition to electronic medical records has added to physicians' frustrations, creating barriers to patient care and collaboration. System-wide reform, including reducing administrative burdens, promoting work-life balance, and implementing tort reform, is essential to address the root causes of burnout.

However, these changes will take time, and coaches are limited in their ability to remediate workplace issues. In the meantime, physicians are left to navigate a toxic system that often drives them to mental illness, addiction, and even early death. Coaching provides a critical means of survival and a pathway to rediscovering joy and meaning in medicine, but coaches can't fix broken systems.

Rediscovering Joy in Medicine

Still, the combination of coaching and peer support may empower physicians to overcome burnout, embrace self-compassion, and thrive. Doctor coaches, many of whom have their own stories of overcoming adversity, offer hope and guidance. Their personal experiences lend authenticity to their coaching as they model resilience and growth. For healthcare practitioners struggling under the weight of burnout and related challenges, reaching out to a doctor coach can be life-changing. Coaching offers a confidential, stigma-free opportunity to heal and grow, restoring the humanity that lies at the heart of medicine.

The Power of Persuasion

*Master these elements of persuasive
communication with patients and colleagues.*

EFFECTIVE COMMUNICATION IS AN ESSENTIAL skill for physicians, whether they are collaborating with colleagues or guiding patients through complex decisions. The art of persuasive conversation — influencing a person's attitudes or behaviors without using force — enables doctors to promote trust, inspire action, and create a shared sense of purpose when employed responsibly and ethically.

Persuasion is distinct from coercion in that the people receiving the message have a choice about whether to act on it. Drawing from the principles of persuasion discussed in psychological works, doctors can enhance their interactions by aligning their communication with the needs, values, and motivations of patients and colleagues.

Purpose: Setting Clear Goals in Medical Conversations

Clarity of purpose is critical when engaging in persuasive communication. Physicians must define their objectives before addressing colleagues or patients. For example, when recommending a treatment plan, a doctor should be specific about the desired outcome, such as improving quality of life or reducing certain risks.

Similarly, during discussions with healthcare teams, clearly articulating the goal of a new protocol ensures alignment and focus. Writing down key points before entering these conversations can help physicians stay on track and make their purpose compelling.

People: Understanding the Audience

Understanding the motivations, fears, and needs of patients and colleagues is the foundation of persuasive dialogue. For patients, this means recognizing their emotional responses, cultural beliefs, and personal goals. A physician discussing the benefits of a lifestyle change, such as quitting smoking, can connect by empathizing with the patient's challenges while highlighting achievable benefits.

With colleagues, understanding their professional priorities — whether it's efficiency, innovation, or patient safety — can guide how recommendations are framed. Taking the time to listen actively cultivates mutual respect and trust, enhancing the likelihood of agreement.

Positioning: Framing the Message Effectively

Framing a message to align with the worldview of the listener is a critical aspect of persuasion. Physicians can present their ideas in ways that resonate deeply with the audience's values. For instance, a suggestion to adopt a new clinical protocol can be positioned as a means to improve patient outcomes and reduce burnout. Similarly, when encouraging patients to adhere to a treatment regimen, framing it as an empowering step toward achieving their personal goals can make the message more relatable. This approach not only secures buy-in but also makes patients and colleagues feel like co-creators of the solution.

Proof: Building Credibility Through Evidence

In medicine, trust is rooted in evidence. To persuade effectively, doctors must support their claims with solid data, logical arguments, and relevant real-world examples. Citing studies, sharing clinical success stories, and presenting concrete outcomes from past interventions lend credibility to recommendations.

For example, when proposing a new surgical technique, providing data on improved patient recovery times and lower complication rates assures colleagues of the benefits. Likewise, for patients, breaking down complex medical evidence into relatable, digestible facts makes the information both persuasive and actionable.

Pathos: Leveraging Emotional Connection

Appealing to emotions can make messages more impactful. Physicians can use stories, imagery, and personal connections to illustrate their points. A doctor advising a hesitant patient to undergo a lifesaving procedure might share an anecdote about a similar case with a positive outcome. When speaking to a team about implementing changes, recounting an emotionally charged patient story can emphasize the urgency and importance of the initiative. Balancing emotional appeals with facts ensures that the message remains virtuous and grounded.

Persistence: Following Through Strategically

Persuasion is not always a single-step process. Persistence, without being overbearing, is crucial in medical contexts where decisions require time and reflection. Doctors can reinforce their messages through strategic follow-ups, such as scheduling additional consultations, providing educational materials, or checking in after initial discussions. A physician encouraging a patient to adopt a healthier lifestyle might share incremental tips and celebrate small victories along the way, maintaining momentum without overwhelming the individual. Persistence demonstrates genuine care and commitment, strengthening the relationship and forging trust.

Psychology: Building on Cialdini's Principles of Influence

The strategies for persuasion outlined in medicine recount fundamental insights from social psychology, particularly those explored in Robert Cialdini's notable book *Influence: The Psychology of Persuasion*. Physicians, whether they realize it or not, often draw upon Cialdini's six principles — authority, reciprocity, commitment, social proof, liking, and scarcity — when communicating with patients and colleagues. By understanding and applying these principles more intentionally, doctors are able to inspire action and collaboration to a greater extent.

For example, the principle of authority is inherent to the physician's role. Patients naturally look to doctors as trusted experts, but authority is strengthened when physicians communicate their recommendations with clarity and confidence backed by evidence. Similarly, reciprocity — the idea that people are inclined to give back when they receive something — can guide patient relationships. A doctor who listens attentively and offers thoughtful advice creates a sense of goodwill, increasing the likelihood that patients will adhere to recommendations.

Cialdini's principle of commitment also has significant implications for medicine. Encouraging patients to take small, actionable steps — such as scheduling a follow-up appointment or setting manageable health goals — builds momentum and reinforces their dedication to improving their health.

Similarly, within a healthcare team, celebrating small wins when implementing a new therapy strengthens collective commitment. Physicians who integrate these psychological principles into their practice are better equipped to enter into stronger partnerships and deliver more effective care.

Cultivating Ethical Persuasion in Medicine

Ultimately, persuasion in medicine must always prioritize the well-being of patients and the integrity of professional relationships. Physicians wield significant influence, and their ability to persuade should be rooted in empathy, transparency, and moral considerations. By mastering these principles, doctors can bridge gaps, resolve conflicts, and raise the level of collaboration in ways that benefit everyone involved.

Through the strategic and compassionate application of persuasive communication, physicians can not only guide patients and colleagues toward better outcomes but also strengthen the human connections that are at the heart of medicine.

Trust in the Doctor-Patient Relationship

A collaborative and supportive environment
for healing and well-being rests on trust.

TRUST IS THE CORNERSTONE OF every strong relationship, and nowhere is this more evident than in the doctor-patient relationship. In this dynamic, trust facilitates open communication, ensures compliance with medical recommendations, and creates a sense of security. However, trust is fragile — hard to earn but easy to lose. Recognizing behaviors that erode trust is essential for maintaining the integrity of this sacred bond.

Honesty: The Bedrock of Trust

A physician's credibility begins with honesty. Patients rely on doctors to provide truthful information, even when the news is difficult to hear. If a doctor withholds or distorts the truth, patients may feel betrayed, compromising their ability to trust future guidance. Just as consistent lying in personal relationships is a red flag, so too is any form of dishonesty in medicine. Patients must feel confident that their doctor will prioritize their well-being over convenience or ego.

Practicing Accountability and Transparency

Trust thrives on accountability and transparency. A doctor who avoids responsibility for mistakes or conceals critical information risks undermining the trust their patients place in them. When patients detect evasive behavior, they may question the doctor's integrity and commitment. Conversely, owning up to errors, being transparent about risks, and communicating openly about treatment options strengthen the doctor-patient bond.

Manipulation and secrecy have no place in the doctor-patient relationship. Just as manipulative behavior in personal interactions destroys trust, doctors who prioritize personal agendas over patient needs erode confidence in their care. Patients must feel that their doctors are advocating for them transparently, without ulterior motives.

Respecting Boundaries and Confidentiality

Respecting patient confidentiality is fundamental to maintaining trust. Much like gossip damages personal relationships, breaching confidentiality can irreparably harm the doctor-patient relationship. Patients need assurance that their vulnerabilities and stories will remain safeguarded. Gossip, whether in social settings or within professional circles, signals a lack of respect for boundaries, casting doubt on the individual's reliability.

Aligning Actions with Words

Consistency between words and actions is critical in fostering trust. When doctors make promises about care but fail to follow through, they risk being perceived as unreliable. For example, if a physician assures a patient that test results will be delivered promptly, but the results are delayed without explanation, the patient's confidence may waver. Patients should feel that their doctors' actions reflect their stated priorities and commitments.

Showing Empathy and Emotional Validation

A physician's ability to empathize and validate a patient's concerns is integral to building trust. Dismissing a patient's feelings or ignoring their perspectives can lead to feelings of neglect and disrespect. Mutual respect is key to any relationship, and in medicine, it ensures that patients feel valued and understood. Without this, the relationship risks becoming transactional, losing its humanistic core.

Leadership and Trust in Healthcare

Doctors, particularly those in leadership roles, must lead by example. Inspirational leaders build trust through integrity and consensus; manipulative leaders who employ tactics like selective communication or blame-shifting erode team morale. Just as patients need trustworthy physicians, healthcare teams require leaders who are open and accountable.

Trust in the doctor-patient relationship is a delicate but vital element of care. Like any strong relationship, it is built on honesty, accountability, respect, and empathy. Dishonesty, avoidance of responsibility, and dismissal of concerns reveal just how important it is for doctors to safeguard the trust they work so hard to earn. In doing so, they not only strengthen their relationships with individual patients but also uphold the broader integrity of the medical profession.

By cultivating trust, doctors can ensure that patients feel secure, respected, and empowered — a foundation upon which healing and connection can flourish.

ESSAY 19

How Doctors Unintentionally Trigger Patient Defensiveness

Certain words and phrases provoke defensive responses
in patients and can have devastating consequences.

IN THE MEDICAL PROFESSION, WORDS matter. Physicians often communicate with good intentions, striving to inform, console, or guide their patients. Yet, despite these intentions, certain common phrases can inadvertently trigger defensiveness or resistance.

When patients feel attacked or dismissed, they stop listening, diverting their focus to self-defense instead of the intended message. This creates barriers to trust, understanding, and collaboration. If words carry such weight, how can doctors shift their language to improve these interactions?

Words That Dismiss Emotions
One of the most problematic phrases is "calm down." While it might seem like a way to diffuse tension, it often comes across as dismissive or patronizing, invalidating the patient's emotions (refer to essay 12). A better approach is acknowledging the feelings at hand by saying, "I can see this matters to you. Help me understand." Such a response not only validates the patient's experience but also bridges a partnership in addressing the issue.

Another phrase that stings is, "You're being too sensitive." This statement suggests weakness and dismisses genuine concerns. Instead, physicians can maintain empathy by saying, "I didn't mean to upset you. Tell me how you feel." This shift opens the door to constructive dialogue, demonstrating respect for the patient's perspective.

Generalizations That Alienate
Phrases like "You always…" or "You never…" are fraught with problems. They generalize specific situations, making patients feel unfairly judged. A more effective alternative is to say, "This reminds

69

me of a pattern. Let's unpack it." By focusing on patterns instead of absolutes, the physician invites the patient to reflect without feeling attacked.

Similarly, "Why would you do that?" often comes across as judgmental and condescending. Replacing it with "I'm curious, what led to that decision?" shifts the tone from criticism to exploration, encouraging openness and mutual understanding.

Statements That Dismiss or Critique

"Let's agree to disagree" might seem like an effective phrase to defuse conflict, but it can feel dismissive, signaling that the conversation isn't worth the effort. A better option is to acknowledge the differing perspectives and say, "We see this differently. Let's find a way forward." This keeps the dialogue collaborative and forward-looking.

Another phrase that can embarrass or alienate patients is, "I would have expected you to know that." This statement implies incompetence and undermines confidence. Instead, a physician can say, "This is nuanced. Let me help clarify it." Such phrasing is supportive and recognizes the complexity of medical knowledge.

Lastly, telling someone, "You're overthinking this," dismisses their concern and undervalues their effort. Reframing the response as "Your detail is great. What if we took a step back?" maintains an appreciation for their input while gently redirecting focus.

The Power of Small Shifts

Small changes in language can lead to dramatic results. When people feel understood, they remain open. And when they stay open, progress becomes possible. The paradox is that by validating emotions, we often diffuse them. Empathy, curiosity, and an even demeanor are the tools to bridge gaps in communication.

This principle extends beyond words. Tone and nonverbal cues, such as facial expressions and body language, can amplify or soften the impact of these phrases. Even tactful wording may trigger defensiveness if delivered with impatience or frustration. Conversely, a relaxed, empathetic tone can transform potentially problematic phrases into opportunities for connection.

Building Trust Through Language

Words have the power to open doors or build walls. By shifting from dismissive or judgmental language to empathetic and curious communication, doctors can build trust and collaboration. This approach doesn't weaken their authority or diminish their expertise; it strengthens the relationship between physician and patient. When we validate emotions and address concerns with understanding, we improve patient outcomes and also reinforce the human connection at the heart of medicine.

The Power of Saying "No" — And Knowing When to Say "Yes"

Learning when and how to say "no" can help set patients' expectations and prevent physician burnout.

IN THE MEDICAL PROFESSION, THE ability to say "no" is often undervalued, yet it is a crucial skill for maintaining balance and achieving personal goals. Physicians, by nature, are inclined to help others, which can lead to an overwhelming sense of obligation to meet every demand placed on them. However, constantly saying "yes" can detract from focusing on what truly matters professionally and personally.

Why Say "No"?

We live in a world where expectations are ever-increasing, and around-the-clock availability is often assumed. This is particularly true in medicine, where the pressure to be perpetually accessible can be immense. Yet, learning to say "no" is about setting boundaries to protect your time and energy. It is not about rejecting every request but rather about discerning which tasks align with your goals and which do not. By doing so, you prioritize your own agenda, ensuring that your aspirations are not sidelined by the demands of others.

Saying "no" can help you reach your goals by freeing up time to focus on your own responsibilities. If you are constantly tending to the needs of colleagues, administrators, or even patients beyond reasonable expectations, you risk neglecting your own career advancements and personal development. For instance, a physician who is always volunteering for extra shifts or administrative tasks may find little time left for continuing education or research projects that could enhance their expertise and career trajectory.

Moreover, saying "no" can increase your effectiveness. Multitasking, especially in an error-prone environment like healthcare, often leads to decreased quality and efficiency. By concentrating on fewer tasks, you can devote more attention to each, improving both your performance and the outcomes for your patients. This focused approach enhances your ability to enter a "flow state" where you can work with maximum concentration and effectiveness.

Additionally, the power of saying "no" can increase your value. When you are constantly available, your contributions can become undervalued. You may be taken for granted. The "Yes Man" principle or the "Yes Person" phenomenon suggests that individuals who are inclined to agree or say "yes" to requests are often given more responsibilities and tasks. This tendency occurs because they are perceived as reliable and willing to take on additional work, which can sometimes lead to an imbalance in workload distribution.

By saying "no" and establishing boundaries, you communicate that your time and expertise are precious. This can lead to greater respect from colleagues and patients alike, making your assistance more meaningful when you do choose to offer it.

Reducing stress is another significant benefit of learning to say "no." The constant pressure to fulfill every request can easily lead to burnout. By limiting the number of tasks you agree to, you reduce the stress associated with over-commitment and ensure that you can deal with your own responsibilities effectively. This preserves your mental health and increases your ability to provide quality care.

Why Say "Yes"?

While saying "no" can be a superpower for physicians, it is equally important to be supportive and collaborative and understand the critical incidents and events that doctors must say "yes" to. One of the most critical instances is in the direct care of patients. This includes responding to urgent medical needs, providing necessary treatments, and ensuring that patients receive timely and appropriate care.

In situations where a patient's health is at risk, a physician's commitment to their well-being takes precedence, and saying "yes" to these responsibilities is essential to uphold sworn oaths and maintain the trust placed in them by patients and their families.

Doctors must also say "yes" to opportunities for continuing education and professional development. The medical field is constantly evolving, with new research, technologies, and treatment guidelines emerging regularly. By agreeing to participate in seminars, workshops, and courses, physicians ensure they remain knowledgeable and skilled in the latest advancements, which is crucial for providing high-quality care. This commitment to lifelong learning is vital for personal growth and the advancement of medical practice.

Effective healthcare delivery often requires collaboration with other healthcare professionals. Physicians must say "yes" to working as part of a multidisciplinary team, which can include nurses, specialists, therapists, and administrative staff. This collaboration is essential for comprehensive patient care, ensuring that all aspects of a patient's health are addressed. By embracing teamwork, doctors can contribute to more cohesive and effective treatment, ultimately improving patient outcomes.

Finally, physicians should say "yes" to roles that involve advocacy and leadership within the healthcare system. Whether the roles involve advocating for patient rights, participating in policy development, or leading quality improvement initiatives, they are crucial for driving positive change in healthcare. By stepping into leadership positions, doctors can influence the direction of healthcare practices and policies, ensuring they align with ethical standards and best serve patient interests.

Conclusion

When I accepted a position at a healthcare organization that prided itself on customer service, I was told: "Never say no without saying yes." This expression is often used to encourage a positive approach to communication, particularly in healthcare and other professional settings. The idea is to frame responses in a way that maintains a constructive and cooperative tone. Instead of outright declining a request or opportunity, one might offer an alternative solution or suggest a compromise. This approach helps maintain relationships and encourages problem-solving while still setting boundaries or addressing limitations.

AI in Primary Care Practice Is a Paradigm Shift

The challenge lies in preserving the
narrative aspect of medicine.

ARTIFICIAL INTELLIGENCE (AI) IS TAKING the world by storm, with its market projected to reach well over $300 billion by 2026. While the technology itself has been around in various forms since the 1950s, the explosion of data and technological advancements in recent decades has driven its exponential growth.

This rapid acceleration has elicited both excitement and concern as individuals and businesses explore AI's potential to revolutionize industries. Nowhere is this more evident than in primary care medicine, where the integration of AI holds promise for transforming patient care, alleviating administrative burdens, and addressing many inefficiencies in healthcare.

Primary care is the cornerstone of the healthcare system. Yet primary care physicians (PCPs) are stretched thin, burdened by mounting administrative tasks and alarmingly high burnout rates, as discussed in several essays in this book. The promise of AI in primary care lies in its potential to serve as an ally — one that optimizes processes, supports decision-making, and redefines the doctor–patient relationship for the better.

Benefits of AI

One of the most significant impacts of AI in primary care is its ability to streamline administrative tasks that consume up to one-fourth of a physician's workday. Ambient, AI-powered tools that generate visit summaries directly into electronic health records (EHR) and assist with diagnostics and clinical note drafting are already making strides in reducing the cognitive load on PCPs. These advancements allow physicians to reclaim valuable time and engage in more meaningful interactions with patients.

Beyond documentation, AI systems can automate other tedious processes, such as eligibility checks, prior authorizations, and referrals, further lightening the administrative burden.

AI is also revolutionizing patient engagement and adherence. By leveraging data analytics, AI systems can provide personalized recommendations and real-time insights to help patients manage chronic conditions, adhere to medication regimens, and engage proactively in their healthcare. This technological support not only empowers patients but also strengthens the foundational doctor–patient relationship — a relationship that, despite fears of AI-driven depersonalization, stands to benefit immensely from the integration of supportive technologies.

Perhaps one of AI's most promising roles is in enhancing clinical decision-making. With the sheer volume of medical knowledge doubling every few months, staying current with best practices is a daunting task for any clinician. AI tools can serve as intelligent reference systems, providing rapid, evidence-based recommendations tailored to the patient at hand.

For example, an AI system could instantly retrieve the latest guidelines for evaluating a thyroid nodule, saving the physician valuable time that could be better spent addressing patient concerns. This real-time access to up-to-date knowledge ensures that care decisions are informed by the most current evidence, improving both diagnostic accuracy and patient outcomes.

AI's ability to enhance diagnostics is especially compelling for patients with undifferentiated symptoms. Machine learning algorithms trained on vast datasets can support PCPs in identifying patterns and generating differential diagnoses.

For example, AI tools have been used to detect diabetic retinopathy with a level of accuracy comparable to specialists, allowing PCPs to provide earlier interventions. Similarly, AI-based symptom checkers can guide patients to appropriate care pathways, alleviating administrative burdens and ensuring timely access to specialists.

AI's ability to synthesize large volumes of data also supports a more holistic approach to patient care. By analyzing EHRs, wearable device data, and other inputs, AI can identify patterns and flag potential risks that might otherwise go unnoticed.

For instance, an AI system might detect medication interactions, social determinants of health, or emerging symptoms that require follow-up, ensuring that no aspect of a patient's health is overlooked. This comprehensive perspective allows PCPs to address the full scope of a patient's needs, providing a deeper level of care that extends beyond the immediate presenting issue.

Hurdles and Challenges

Despite these advantages, the implementation of AI in primary care is not without challenges. Fragmented healthcare data, a lack of interoperability between systems, and potential biases in AI algorithms pose significant hurdles. Moreover, the ethical concerns around data privacy and the "black box" nature of some AI models underscore the importance of transparency and accountability.

A model that predicts a patient's likelihood of developing a chronic disease, for instance, may produce accurate results but fail to explain the reasoning behind its prediction — a gap that could undermine trust between patients and physicians.

The narrative dimension of primary care also raises questions about AI's role in the doctor–patient relationship. Primary care is built on stories — the stories patients tell about their symptoms, fears, and lives, and the stories clinicians construct to make sense of these narratives within a clinical framework.

AI may help process and organize these stories, but it cannot replicate the empathy, intuition, and human connection that form the bedrock of primary care. As tools like chatbots and virtual assistants become more sophisticated, clinicians must ensure that the use of AI accentuates rather than diminishes these essential elements of care.

The Essence of the Story

A practical example illustrates this tension. Imagine an AI assistant identifying a patient's symptoms as consistent with a rare genetic disorder. The system provides an accurate diagnosis but misses the essence of the patient's story: how their symptoms impact their daily life, their family dynamics, and their mental health. Without these details, the care plan risks being disconnected from the patient's lived experience.[1]

Here, the physician's role as a "storykeeper" becomes indispensable, as a major shortcoming of AI is its failure to fully extract clinical information on question-answering tasks. Tasks such as summarization, conversational dialogue, and translation remain underexplored by large language models.

The future of AI in primary care lies in collaboration. Clinicians and data scientists must work together to create systems that are not only effective but also realistic and empathetic. By integrating AI thoughtfully into primary care, PCPs can improve diagnostic precision and streamline workflows for patients while preserving the narrative heart of medicine.

REFERENCE

1. Bedi S, Liu Y, Orr-Ewing L, Dash D, *et al*. Testing and Evaluation of Health Applications of Large Language Models: A Systematic Review. *JAMA*. 2025;333(4):319–328. doi:10.1001/jama.2024.21700

The Five-Star Dilemma of Patient Ratings

Doctors' ratings may encompass experiences beyond their control.

THE RISE OF PATIENT RATING systems has given consumers more input into healthcare, influencing everything from physician compensation to institutional rankings. These systems, championed by companies like Press Ganey, claim to enhance the patient experience by providing a voice to those receiving care. However, their fairness and impact on medical decision-making remain contentious topics among healthcare professionals.

On the one hand, patient feedback is a valuable tool. Patients are the ultimate recipients of healthcare services, and their experiences matter. A compassionate, communicative doctor who listens attentively and explains medical decisions thoroughly should be recognized and rewarded. In an ideal world, ratings would reflect these qualities, helping other patients find competent and caring physicians. Moreover, ratings can incentivize doctors to refine their bedside manner, improving the overall patient experience.

However, in practice, physician rating systems often create unintended consequences. Many doctors feel pressured to "play the game" to maintain high scores, sometimes at the expense of sound medical judgment. If a patient expects unnecessary cardiac testing or demands an antibiotic for a viral infection, a doctor who refuses may risk a poor review, while another who obliges receives high marks.

This dynamic can lead to excessive medical testing, over-prescription of medications, and increased healthcare costs — all to appease patient expectations rather than adhere to best medical practices. Before you know it, doctors will be behaving like salespeople, forewarning customers to give them five-star ratings on follow-up surveys.

The financial interests behind rating systems further complicate their validity. Press Ganey, for example, is a for-profit company valued at over $4.25 billion. Its business model thrives on selling its survey services to healthcare institutions, which, in turn, use these ratings to evaluate their physicians.

In today's competitive healthcare market, patient experience is more important than ever. It's the key to building trust and loyalty. Unfortunately for doctors, it's more than just good bedside manner — the true patient experience encompasses everything from appointment booking to follow-up communications and more. Whether they like it or not, physicians are often on the hook for patient experiences that extend beyond the "four walls."

Hospitals increasingly tie physician compensation and career advancement to patient satisfaction scores, creating a system where doctors may feel pressured to prioritize popularity over sound clinical decision-making. Unlike corporate executives, who can brush off a poor review, physicians face tangible repercussions, including reduced compensation, difficulty securing promotions, and added stress in an already high-burnout profession.

That said, some argue that physicians should not be so concerned about ratings. A doctor who genuinely listens, educates, and engages patients will likely receive strong reviews regardless of occasional outliers. A one-star rating from a disgruntled patient demanding unnecessary tests should not overshadow the many positive reviews from those who appreciate thoughtful, evidence-based care. Physicians who focus on building trust and communication can overcome the negative effects of the system by ensuring patients understand the reasoning behind medical decisions.

Ultimately, the fairness of patient ratings depends on how they are used. When viewed in context, they can be a helpful, albeit imperfect, measure of patient experience. However, when tied to financial incentives and job security, they risk distorting medical decision-making. Physicians should not have to choose between doing what is right and securing a high rating.

Perhaps the solution lies in shifting healthcare priorities — directing resources away from corporate-driven rating systems and toward meaningful patient care. Until then, doctors must understand this reality, balancing patient satisfaction with their ethical duty to provide appropriate, evidence-based medicine.

When Ratings Go Bad

Physicians who find themselves on the receiving end of unfair or misleading reviews do have options to contest them. While it may be impossible to eliminate every unwarranted negative rating, there are concrete steps doctors can take to protect their reputations and ensure a fairer portrayal of their practice.

First, doctors should monitor their online presence regularly. Platforms like Google, Healthgrades, and WebMD allow patients to leave reviews, and being aware of what is being said can help physicians address concerns proactively. If a review contains false or defamatory information — such as an accusation of misconduct or an outright lie about the treatment provided — doctors can often request its removal.

Google, for example, has guidelines against defamatory or misleading content, and WebMD allows providers to dispute certain types of reviews. Physicians should familiarize themselves with each platform's policies and submit formal requests when appropriate.

Second, while patient privacy laws such as HIPAA prevent physicians from responding to reviews with specifics about a case, they can provide a general professional response to counteract misleading impressions. A well-crafted response that maintains professionalism, such as "We take all feedback seriously and strive to provide evidence-based care. We encourage patients to discuss concerns directly with us to ensure the best possible experience," can demonstrate to future readers that the physician is attentive and patient-centered.

Another strategy is to encourage satisfied patients to leave reviews but not mandate it. The reality of online ratings is that unhappy patients are often more vocal than satisfied ones. A doctor with a solid patient base can gently remind those who express gratitude for their care that they are welcome to share their experiences online. This helps create a more balanced and accurate reflection of a physician's practice.

Physicians can also reach out to their hospital or employer's administrative team if they believe their ratings are being unfairly weaponized against them. If a healthcare system is using Press Ganey scores to determine compensation or promotion, doctors should advocate for a more hands-on evaluation system that takes into account the limitations and biases inherent in patient satisfaction ratings. Institutions that truly value their clinicians should recognize that good medicine sometimes involves making unpopular decisions.

Remember the Ultimate Goal

Ultimately, while physicians cannot entirely escape the influence of patient ratings, they can take steps to manage their reputations and push back against an unfair system. By monitoring reviews, disputing false claims, crafting professional responses, encouraging satisfied patients to contribute their perspectives, and advocating for fairer institutional policies, doctors can protect both their integrity and their ability to practice sound, ethical medicine.

The goal should always be to provide the best care possible, not to chase five-star ratings at the expense of medical judgment.

Why Physicians Need Business Education

Learning the language of business has become as
important as learning the language of medicine.

MEDICAL EDUCATION HAS LONG BEEN compromised by the conspic-
uous absence of business training. Medical schools, the Association
of American Medical Colleges (AAMC), and related administrative
entities have historically avoided incorporating business education
into their curriculums, citing an already overcrowded curriculum.
This omission perpetuates the myth that physicians do not need
business knowledge to practice medicine.

Yet a survey of over 500 first- through fourth-year medical
students revealed that more than half would be "very likely" or
"somewhat likely" to take a business and medicine course during
medical school if offered, believing this education was important:
90% had "no," "minimal," or "basic" perceived knowledge of the
field.[1]

Medical students are indoctrinated into believing that clinical
expertise alone is sufficient, a belief reinforced by the lack of discussion on business topics throughout their training. Consequently, most
physicians enter practice business-illiterate, unprepared to manage the
operational, financial, and marketing aspects of a medical practice,
and vulnerable to the economic pitfalls of independent practice.

The deliberate exclusion of business education is not only a
glaring omission but a disservice to physicians. Despite the overwhelming evidence from other industries that business principles
are critical to success, medical schools continue to propagate the
idea that business acumen is unnecessary or should be obtained later.

This systematic neglect leaves physicians unprepared to navigate
the financial realities of their profession, and many are blindsided by
the economic pressures of private practice. The result is a staggering
attrition rate among private practice physicians and the continued

erosion of independent medical practice as a viable career path — approximately 75% of all physicians today are employees of hospitals or health systems.[2]

The Consequences of Business Ignorance

Physicians in private practice face unique challenges that demand a solid understanding of business principles. These include managing cash flow, understanding revenue cycles, optimizing operational efficiency, and effectively marketing their services — not to mention the less traditional but equally important "softer" skills of business such as human resources and strategic management.

Yet, the overwhelming majority of physicians graduate without any formal business training, leaving them ill-equipped to sustain and grow their practices. This lack of preparation is evident in the high failure rate of private practices, mirroring the struggles faced by small businesses that fail due to poor financial management and inadequate marketing strategies.

For physicians, the economic realities of private practice are further exacerbated by systemic changes in healthcare, such as the rise of government-controlled (or regulated) facilities, HMOs and PPOs, and equity-backed investor ownership. These developments have siphoned patients from independent practices, leaving many physicians struggling to compete. Without the necessary business knowledge, physicians often find themselves unable to adapt, leading to financial hardship, practice closures, or forced employment in corporate-like settings.

The Need for a Paradigm Shift in Medical Education

To address this crisis, medical education must undergo a fundamental shift. Business education should be integrated into the medical school curriculum as an essential component of training. Offering business courses during medical school, when students are most receptive to learning, would equip future physicians with the tools they need to succeed in practice. Without the tools to effectively manage and market their services, many physicians find themselves unable to compete with larger, non-physician-owned medical businesses.

Business education for physicians need not be overly complex or time-consuming. A well-designed program, a distillation of the most important concepts taught in MBA programs, could provide practical, actionable knowledge suited to the unique needs of medical professionals. A tailored business education integrated into medical training would provide future physicians with the necessary skills to thrive in an increasingly competitive and complex healthcare environment.

For those in private practice, such training could mean the difference between financial stability and insolvency. Understanding business principles would empower physicians to take control of their careers, reduce burnout, and improve patient care by ensuring the sustainability of their practices. Moreover, it would provide physicians a seat at the table alongside the "suits."

For physicians like me, who came to realize the importance of business principles after medical school, it's still not too late to be educated. Executive MBA programs are designed for working professionals — physicians and non-physicians — and can be completed in two years or less. This education can empower physicians to better advocate for patient care and contribute to the operational success of their practices. *MD/MBA: Physicians on the New Frontier of Medical Management* is a definitive resource of information about education for effective physician leadership.[3]

Reclaiming the Profession's Future

The myth that physicians can practice medicine without understanding business has contributed significantly to the current crisis in healthcare. The attrition of private practice physicians, the increasing corporatization of medicine, and the financial struggles many face in the profession are all symptoms of a deeper problem: the failure to equip physicians with the knowledge and skills they need to succeed. Physicians need to understand and talk the language of business equally as well as they have come to understand and talk the language of medicine.

Business education is not a luxury; it is a necessity. The intersection of medicine and business is undeniable, and the need for business education in medical training is urgent. By integrating business principles into medical training, we can enable physicians to reclaim their autonomy, sustain their practices, and provide high-quality care.

The time has come to challenge the status quo, dispel the myths, and ensure that future generations of physicians are not only skilled clinicians but also savvy business leaders. As we move forward, medical schools must recognize the value of business education and integrate it into their curricula. In doing so, we can secure the future of independent medical practice and preserve the profession's integrity for years to come.

REFERENCES

1. Natanov D, Tringali S, Muratori J, and Shain S. The Business of Healing: Medical Students' Opinions on the Need for Formal Business Training in the Medical School Curriculum. *Physician Leadership Journal*. 2024; 11(6):10–16. https://www.physicianleaders.org/articles/doi/10.55834/plj.6704136676.
2. Physicians Advocacy Institute. Updated Report: Hospital and Corporate Acquisition of Physician Practices and Physician Employment 2019–2023. April 2024. https://www.physiciansadvocacyinstitute.org/PAI-Research/PAI-Avalere-Study-on-Physician-Employment-Practice-Ownership-Trends-2019-2023.
3. Lazarus A, ed. *MD/MBA: Physicians on the New Frontier of Medical Management*. American College of Physician Executives; 1998.

ESSAY 24

Affirmative Action in Medicine's New Era

The long-standing debate over merit versus identity
takes a new turn — with uncertain results.

THE 2023 SUPREME COURT'S LANDMARK ruling in *Students for Fair Admissions (SFFA) v. Harvard*, combined with President Trump's executive order targeting the elimination of diversity, equity, and inclusion (DEI) practices, signals a seismic shift in medical education, healthcare institutions, and federal grantmaking. Together, these initiatives aim to enforce race-neutral policies in areas historically shaped by affirmative action and DEI initiatives, prompting significant ramifications for admissions, hiring, and funding practices within the medical field.

Medical School Admissions: Upholding Merit in a Post-*SFFA* Era

The *SFFA* decision declared race-conscious admissions practices unconstitutional, asserting that such policies violate the Equal Protection Clause and Title VI of the Civil Rights Act. Trump's executive order amplifies this ruling by ensuring universities, including medical schools, comply with the *SFFA* decision.[1] The stakes are particularly high in medical education, where affirmative action policies have long influenced admissions decisions.

However, many medical schools appear to be circumventing the ruling. Disparities in academic metrics — such as MCAT scores and GPAs — persist among matriculants of different racial and ethnic backgrounds. Furthermore, highly talented White and Asian students have been denied medical school admission and have claimed "reverse" discrimination. Despite the Court's ruling, some schools continue to prioritize DEI initiatives under the guise of "holistic admissions," raising questions about their commitment to merit-based evaluations.

87

Trump's executive order underscores the need for rigorous enforcement. By mandating federal oversight and tying compliance to funding, the administration aims to dismantle practices that prioritize racial quotas over academic excellence. This shift could restore trust in medical school admissions by ensuring that all applicants are evaluated on their qualifications rather than their race.

DEI in the Private Sector: Impact on Medical Associations

The executive order's reach extends beyond academic institutions to private organizations, including medical associations. Federal agencies are tasked with identifying and investigating the most egregious DEI practices in the private sector, with an explicit focus on medical societies. This scrutiny appears to be warranted, according to the Trump administration, as organizations such as the Association of American Medical Colleges (AAMC) have been at the forefront of embedding DEI principles into many aspects of medical education, from curriculum design to hiring practices.

Medical associations have continued to promote racially conscious policies, often through scholarships and opportunities that explicitly favor certain racial or ethnic groups. Such practices not only undermine the principle of equity but also risk alienating talented individuals who feel sidelined by identity-based preferences. The executive order's emphasis on eradicating discriminatory DEI initiatives in private organizations aims to realign these entities with the principles of merit and fairness.

Federal Grantmaking: Removing DEI Bias

A pivotal aspect of Trump's executive order involves eliminating DEI language and practices from federal contracting and grantmaking processes. Federal agencies like the National Institutes of Health (NIH) have been criticized for prioritizing diversity over merit in research funding decisions. Grant applications explicitly favored certain racial groups, leading to accusations of bias and inefficiency.

By excising DEI mandates from grantmaking criteria, the executive order seeks to streamline the funding process and ensure that grants are awarded based on scientific merit rather than identity politics. This approach could enhance innovation and excellence in medical research, benefitting both practitioners and patients by prioritizing outcomes over optics.

Broader Implications for Healthcare

These changes carry enormous implications for the healthcare system. Proponents argue that enforcing race-neutral policies will elevate standards and restore public trust in medical institutions. Critics, however, warn that these measures may exacerbate existing disparities in healthcare access and outcomes, particularly for historically underserved communities.

The tension between these perspectives underscores the need for a balanced approach. While the pursuit of equity is a laudable goal, it must not come at the expense of excellence or the ethical imperative to provide the best possible care to all patients. The executive order's focus on merit and fairness seeks to strike this balance, though its success will ultimately depend on transparent implementation and vigilant oversight.

A Turning Point for Medicine

The intersection of the *SFFA* ruling and Trump's executive order marks a turning point for the medical field. By challenging the entrenched norms of affirmative action and DEI, these initiatives aim to refocus medical education and practice on the principles of merit, excellence, and equality under the law. However, resistance to these changes remains widespread, with many educators concerned that the Trump administration's stance toward DEI will have negative medical sequelae — not only for the future composition of doctors but for other areas such as health coverage, global health, and gender identity (see the next essay).

As the healthcare community settles into this new landscape, it must grapple with complex questions about diversity, equity, and the role of merit in medicine. Ultimately, the success of these reforms will hinge on their ability to sculpt a system that is both fair and effective, ensuring that the next generation of medical professionals is prepared to meet the challenges of an increasingly complex world and still be committed to tackling the problem of health disparities.

REFERENCE

1. Exec. Order No. 14173, 90 Fed. Reg. 8633 (Jan 21, 2025). https://www.federalregister.gov/documents/2025/01/31/2025-02097/ending-illegal-discrimination-and-restoring-merit-based-opportunity

Executive Orders on Gender Identity and DEI Programs

*Rolling back transgender protections and DEI programs
could have chilling effects on population health.*

THE EXECUTIVE ORDERS SIGNED BY President Donald Trump on his first day back in office signal a dramatic shift in federal policy regarding transgender rights and diversity, equity, and inclusion (DEI) programs that are bound to affect clinical practice. These policies, framed as efforts to end "social engineering" in public and private life, also have significant implications for public health and the broader societal approach to equity.

While proponents hail these moves as protecting traditional values and advancing a merit-based society, critics argue they roll back hard-won civil rights and jeopardize the well-being of vulnerable populations.

Impact on Transgender Health and Care Access

The order to define sex strictly as male or female based on reproductive cells present at conception has significant implications for healthcare delivery. By excluding nonbinary, intersex, and transgender identities from recognition in federal policies and documents, this move conflicts with scientific consensus. The American Medical Association and American Psychiatric Association have long affirmed that gender is a spectrum, supported by extensive research on biological, psychological, and social dimensions of identity.

For transgender individuals, these changes could mean:

1. **Restricted Access to Gender-Affirming Care:** The prohibition on federal funds for transition-related services, including hormones and surgeries, directly limits access for low-income individuals reliant on Medicaid. While existing state-level Medicaid policies may remain in place, federal resistance could embolden states to restrict coverage further.

2. **Barriers to Legal Recognition:** Removing gender marker options, such as the "X" designation on passports, complicates everyday interactions for transgender and nonbinary individuals, from employment to healthcare access. Without accurate identification, patients may face delays or denials in accessing gender-sensitive care.

3. **Increased Vulnerability in Prisons:** Federal prisons house nearly 2,300 transgender inmates — about 1.5% of the total population. Housing transgender inmates based on sex assigned at birth rather than gender identity raises significant safety concerns. Transgender women in men's prisons face heightened risks of assault and isolation. The halting of gender-affirming medical care within federal prisons exacerbates these vulnerabilities, undermining efforts to address the mental and physical health needs of incarcerated individuals.

Healthcare Workforce and DEI Programs

The simultaneous termination of DEI initiatives within federal agencies has ripple effects across the healthcare workforce and patient outcomes. DEI programs aim to address disparities in access to care, improve cultural competency, and promote inclusion for historically marginalized groups, including racial and gender minorities.

By dismantling these programs, the administration risks several negative consequences:

1. **Widening Health Disparities:** DEI initiatives help address the social determinants of health, such as racism and gender discrimination, that contribute to inequities in outcomes. Removing these efforts may exacerbate disparities, particularly for communities already facing barriers to care.

2. **Decreased Workforce Diversity:** A diverse healthcare workforce is critical to delivering equitable care. Studies show that providers from underrepresented backgrounds are more likely to serve medically underserved communities. Without DEI efforts, recruiting and retaining diverse talent may become more challenging, further marginalizing these populations.

3. **Chilling Effect on Private Sector Efforts:** The rollback of federal DEI programs could influence private institutions, which often model their initiatives on federal policies. As seen with corporations like Walmart and Meta scaling back diversity policies post-election, federal disapproval may lead to a broader retreat from equity-focused work in the private sector, affecting access and inclusion nationwide.

Legal and Ethical Concerns

Many provisions of these executive orders will likely face legal challenges, given their tension with established laws and constitutional protections. For example:

- The rollback of transgender protections in prisons and Medicaid could conflict with constitutional guarantees of equal protection under the law and court rulings affirming the rights of transgender individuals to access care.
- The framing of DEI initiatives as discriminatory against majority groups echoes legal debates surrounding affirmative action and may lead to further litigation.

Moreover, these policies raise ethical concerns about the government's role in advancing or undermining health equity. Healthcare is a fundamental human right, and policies that limit access or recognition based on identity challenge the principles of justice and beneficence that underpin medical ethics.

Public Health and Societal Implications

Beyond individual healthcare access, these orders carry broader public health consequences. Policies that stigmatize transgender individuals and undermine DEI efforts contribute to minority stress, a well-documented driver of poor mental and physical health outcomes. The erosion of protections could lead to increased rates of depression, anxiety, and suicide among transgender and nonbinary people, as well as reduced trust in healthcare institutions.

Additionally, by marginalizing diverse groups, these policies risk polarizing society further and undermining social cohesion. The rollback of DEI efforts, particularly the irony of signing the executive order on Martin Luther King Jr. Day, sends a symbolic message that many perceive as a step backward in the nation's ongoing pursuit of equality. For healthcare professionals, policymakers, and advocates, the road ahead will involve navigating legal battles, mitigating harm to affected populations, and continuing to champion equity and inclusion in both public policy and medical practice.

Andrew F. Beck, MD, MPH, a pediatrician at Cincinnati Children's Hospital Medical Center, observed, "We can no longer fully separate the practice of medicine from politics and policy. Rather, we can come to this intersection with evidence, objectivity, empathy, curiosity, humility, and a dedication to what is right and just. Whether it be calling an elected official or even running to unseat them, we most certainly can and should use our voice today, tomorrow, and all the days to come."[2]

Indeed, there are dozens of lawsuits challenging executive orders that Trump issued within hours of his second inauguration. DEI is at a crossroads, and the future path remains unclear. A recalibration — one that reaffirms a commitment to scientific integrity and high standards while acknowledging the need for a diverse and inclusive medical agenda — is necessary. Ideology and excellence don't have to be mutually exclusive.

REFERENCES

1. Exec. Order 14168, 90 Fed. Reg. 8615 (Jan. 20, 2025). https://www.federalregister.gov/documents/2025/01/30/2025-02090/defending-women-from-gender-ideology-extremism-and-restoring-biological-truth-to-the-federal.
2. Beck AF. Election Night. *JAMA*. 2025;333(3):205–206. doi:10.1001/jama.2024.25200

Practicing Medicine in the Rainbow State Is Not as Colorful as It Appears

*Hawai'i's physician shortage reflects
a national healthcare crisis.*

I RECEIVED A LETTER FROM a professor in the Department of Family Medicine of the John A. Burns School of Medicine at the University of Hawai'i, Honolulu. The letter read, "Aloha! I don't think you live in Hawai'i, but you do have a license here, so there is no reason you couldn't be living here in paradise! We have lots of great jobs, opportunities for locums, and even loan repayment for everyone, including subspecialists. We are a very safe place to live, and we are free to practice our full scope of care here. Here is a link to job postings that we update regularly, and attached is our latest physician workforce report showing that we need you!!"

Clicking on the website link[1] revealed content that invited me to explore an enticing vision of life and work, encouraging me to see how the aloha lifestyle aligns with my personal and professional goals. The website stated that "[f]resh fish, choice waves, and a short drive to Auntie's house are just a few of the perks of practicing in Hawai'i... Once you're off of work, go surfing, try that new restaurant, or just stop off for some *poke* for the family on your way home."

The truth is, I'm not a huge fan of poke (diced raw fish), and there is a downside to practicing in the rainbow state — the extraordinarily high cost of living and real estate, which is not offset by salary. I was on the professor's list because, although I do hold a Hawai'i medical license, I only go to Hawai'i to vacation and visit family. I maintain my license just in case I move there to practice or teach at the medical school. Many other physicians appear to have similar thoughts in that approximately two of three doctors who have a Hawai'i medical license are not active.

Nationwide Physician Shortage

Hawai'i presents a particularly acute example of the nationwide physician shortage crisis, with projections indicating that the United States could face a deficit of up to 139,000 physicians by 2033. The *Hawai'i Physician Workforce Assessment Project*, completed in December 2024, showed that despite over 12,000 licensed physicians in the state, only 3,672 actively provide patient care, equating to approximately 3,075 full-time equivalents (FTEs).[2]

The state requires 3,618 FTEs to meet demand, leaving a shortfall of 543 FTEs, which rises to 768 FTEs when geographic distribution challenges are factored in. This shortage is exacerbated by an aging population nationwide requiring more medical care and an aging physician workforce where nearly a quarter of physicians are already 65 or older.

Regional Disparities and Specialty Deficits

The physician shortage is not uniformly distributed across Hawai'i; some counties (islands) experience more severe deficits than others. Primary care remains the most critical area of shortage, with a statewide deficit of 152 FTEs. Additionally, subspecialties such as pediatric gastroenterology, pulmonology, endocrinology, colorectal surgery, and thoracic surgery face some of the highest percentage shortages, with some specialties experiencing deficits of more than 80%. Emergency medicine, intensive care, and psychiatry also show significant gaps, reflecting the broader national trend where mental health and critical care services are in high demand but lack adequate workforce support.

Factors Contributing to Physician Shortages

Several factors contribute to the ongoing physician shortage. Low physician reimbursement rates, particularly in Medicare and Medicaid services, make private practice financially unsustainable for many doctors. Hawai'i's high cost of living, combined with the state's general excise tax, places additional financial strain on physicians, particularly those in private practice.

Additionally, administrative burdens such as complex prior authorization requirements, electronic health record inefficiencies, and extensive credentialing processes deter physicians from remaining in practice or moving to states like Hawai'i. Physician burnout, a long-standing issue that was exacerbated by the COVID-19 pandemic, has led to increased retirement rates and declining mental health among healthcare providers.

Solutions to Address Physician Shortages

Efforts to alleviate the physician shortage in Hawai'i have included a range of recruitment and retention initiatives. The state has launched the Hawai'i Healthcare Education Loan Repayment Program (HELP), allocating $30 million to help repay student loans for 800 healthcare workers, making practice in Hawai'i more financially viable for new graduates. Legislative efforts have also successfully exempted healthcare providers from the general excise tax on public insurance payments, providing some financial relief to struggling practices.

Increasing reimbursement rates for Medicare and Medicaid services remains a top priority. Advocacy efforts, including the "Protecting Access to Care in Hawai'i (PATCH)" Act, aim to raise reimbursement rates to levels similar to those in Alaska, making Hawai'i a more attractive location for medical professionals. Additionally, targeted financial incentives such as state tax credits, reduced mortgage rates, and four-day workweeks have been identified as key factors that could encourage physicians to relocate to Hawai'i.

Leveraging Telehealth and Administrative Reforms

Telehealth expansion has played a crucial role in bridging gaps in healthcare access, particularly for rural and underserved communities. The Physician Workforce Research team has worked to integrate electronic health record improvements, enhance broadband access in rural areas, and offer free telemental health services. Efforts to simplify prior authorization processes and reduce administrative burdens could also alleviate physician workload, increasing job satisfaction and retention rates.

Building a Sustainable Healthcare Workforce

Long-term solutions must focus on pipeline development, ensuring a steady influx of trained healthcare professionals, as well as retaining medical school graduates and residents, many of whom leave the state for higher-paying opportunities on the mainland. Initiatives such as the Hawai'i Preceptor Tax Credit incentivize experienced physicians to mentor medical students and residents, helping cultivate the next generation of doctors.

The Bridge to Practice program connects residents with independent practices, encouraging them to establish careers in Hawai'i. Additionally, high school certification programs and teen health camps aim to introduce young students to healthcare careers early, fostering interest and engagement in the medical field.

Conclusion

Hawai'i's physician shortage is severe yet not dissimilar from other states. The solution requires a combination of financial incentives, administrative reforms, telehealth expansion, and workforce pipeline development. While progress has been made in Hawai'i through initiatives like loan repayment programs, tax exemptions, and recruitment efforts, continued legislative support and innovative changes are needed to ensure a sustainable healthcare workforce. Addressing these challenges is critical not only for Hawai'i but also for the broader U.S. healthcare system, as physician shortages continue to impact access to care nationwide.

REFERENCE

1. John A. Burns School of Medicine Healthcare Job Board. University of Hawai'i. https://ahec.hawaii.edu/ahecsite-forhealthcareprofessionals/healthcare-job-board.html.
2. University of Hawai'i. Report to the 2025 Legislature. Annual Report on Findings from the Hawai'i Physician Workforce Assessment Project. December 2024. https://www.hawaii.edu/govrel/docs/reports/2025/act18-sslh2009_2025_physician-workforce_annual-report_508.pdf.

Section 2

CAREER

∞

Is Medicine a Calling or a Career?

Balancing dedication, well-being, and patient care in a changing profession.

THE QUESTION OF WHETHER MEDICINE is a calling or a job divides the profession and reflects generational shifts in attitudes toward work and life balance. Historically, physicians endured long hours and rigorous demands, often sacrificing personal well-being to prioritize patient care. This mindset was seen as an essential component of the profession, binding doctors in a shared culture of dedication.

Today, however, a new wave of medical practitioners challenges this perspective, seeking a balance that accommodates both professional commitment and personal fulfillment. Unlike physicians of yesteryear who accepted being at the mercy of their pagers, young doctors are questioning medicine's workaholic culture, demanding a better work-life balance.

Challenges of the Sandwich Generation

Younger physicians emphasize the importance of self-care, arguing that sustainable work practices are necessary to provide high-quality care. Many balance demanding careers with responsibilities at home, such as parenting or caring for aging relatives.

The term "sandwich generation" describes individuals who care simultaneously for aging parents and children, representing about a quarter of all adults in the United States. These caregivers often face financial and emotional difficulty; feelings of depression, guilt, and isolation; and trouble managing work, hobbies, and relationships. For physicians, caregiver burnout may compound the exhaustion associated with patient care.

Burnout and Bureaucracy

Despite advancements like shorter working hours and tools to alleviate administrative tasks, burnout persists at a high level. Critics of the current system suggest that the root of this dissatisfaction may not lie solely in overwork but in a lack of meaningful connection with patients. For some, practicing medicine within corporate frameworks feels more like fulfilling tasks than fulfilling a vocation.

Physicians increasingly work as employees of health systems, where administrative burdens, electronic documentation, and insurance battles detract from the satisfaction of direct patient care. Conversely, those who regain autonomy through private practice or specialized roles often rediscover a sense of purpose, even with long hours.

Generational Expectations

The debate extends to generational attitudes. Earlier generations often worked tirelessly under the belief that medicine demanded total commitment. While some express frustration with shifting attitudes, they also acknowledge modern constraints, such as increased bureaucracy and declining reimbursements.

Younger practitioners advocate for systems that respect boundaries and time away from work, arguing that professional identity and personal well-being are not mutually exclusive.

Balancing Technology and Humanity

Technology offers potential solutions. Innovations like AI transcription tools reduce time spent on documentation, allowing more focus on clinical care. However, challenges like rising costs, inefficiencies, and liability concerns persist.

Ultimately, medicine's transformation reflects its dual nature as both a profession and a personal journey. Bridging the divide requires respecting diverse approaches and finding common ground to meet the needs of both practitioners and patients.

Patients' Perspectives on Calling vs. Career

From the patient's viewpoint, the question of whether medicine is a calling or a job carries significant implications. Patients often seek not only clinical expertise but also empathy, reassurance, and continuity. For many, the ideal physician is one who views their work as a calling — someone deeply invested in their well-being and willing to go the extra mile.

However, modern healthcare's emphasis on teamwork and efficiency has shifted expectations. For instance, a patient in an emergency values around-the-clock availability over an individual doctor's personal dedication.

Nuances in Patient Expectations

Patients appreciate the idealism of doctors who see their work as a vocation, especially for chronic or complex conditions. Yet, they also value professionalism, competency, and respect for boundaries. Attributes like accessibility, clear communication, and coordinated care are often prioritized over physicians sacrificing personal balance.

Interestingly, studies show that empathy, active listening, and clear communication matter more to patients than technical expertise alone. These qualities are not exclusive to those who view medicine as a calling but can also be cultivated by those who approach their work with professionalism and emotional intelligence.

Blending Strengths for Better Outcomes

A healthcare system that combines the strengths of both perspectives benefits patients the most. Physicians who view medicine as a calling may inspire confidence and deliver deeply personal care, while those who see it as a structured job may offer efficiency and adaptability.

Patients do not require their doctors to sacrifice their personal lives; they need a system that enables compassionate, high-quality care without burnout.

Competence, Connection, and Compassion

As healthcare evolves, patients may care less about whether their doctor views medicine as a calling or a career. Instead, they demand a health system capable of delivering both empathy and effectiveness, ensuring physicians can remain present and compassionate without compromising their own well-being.

In the end, patients seek what all people desire from those who care for them: competence, connection, and compassion — however it is achieved.

Brutal Career Truths for Doctors (Read This Before It's Too Late)

Understand these truths to accelerate your career.

CAREERS IN MEDICINE ARE UNIQUELY demanding, offering both personal fulfillment and daunting challenges. For physicians at any stage — from students to residents to attendings — understanding the realities of professional life can mean the difference between thriving and fading away. Here are some essential truths every doctor should grasp.

1. Hard work alone doesn't guarantee recognition or success.
Your contributions must be visible. Advocate for yourself and build a reputation for results, not just long hours. Similarly, while loyalty to an employer might feel virtuous, it won't pay the bills. Hospitals and health systems prioritize budgets over individuals, so protecting your interests and personal well-being must come first.

2. Titles in medicine are temporary, and roles often shift.
Whether you're a resident, fellow, or specialist, focus on skill-building and adaptability rather than clinging to status. At the same time, remember that even leaders make mistakes (see essay 53). Respectfully challenge authority when patient care or ethical integrity is at stake. This balance is crucial to maintaining professional integrity.

3. Networking is non-negotiable in medicine.
Expertise opens doors, but relationships keep them open. Collaborate with colleagues, join professional groups, and seek mentorship — these connections can make or break your career trajectory. Yet, in striving for success, avoid falling into the trap of burnout.

Working until you drop isn't noble; it's dangerous. Protect your mental and physical health by delegating and setting boundaries. Remember: an unwell physician cannot heal others effectively. They also contribute to the suboptimal performance of healthcare systems.

4. Comfort zones can stifle growth.

Embrace challenging cases, leadership roles, or even new specialties to expand your horizons. Constructive feedback, though sometimes difficult to hear, is another powerful tool for growth. Learn to discern useful advice from noise and use it to refine your practice.

That said, no matter how skilled or essential you feel, remember that every physician is replaceable. Focus on creating an impact that endures beyond your tenure rather than clinging to irreplaceability.

5. Perfectionism, while often praised, can slow you down in medicine.

Strive for excellence, but don't let perfectionism paralyze your progress. Sometimes, "good enough" is all you need when it's safe and ethical. Career paths in medicine are rarely linear. Detours — such as switching specialties, taking a sabbatical, or moving into administrative roles — can enrich your journey and open unexpected doors.

6. Your career is ultimately your responsibility.

Seek out opportunities, advocate for better conditions, and don't wait for permission to pursue your goals. Things can always get worse, so expect setbacks and plan for them. Have a "plan B." Resilience comes from preparation and adaptability.

Consider yourself the CEO of your own career — a "company of one." Let your core competencies report to you, and you report to your board of mentors. You must manage your own career. Don't depend on serendipity or think that things will automatically fall in line because it is "meant to be." Avoid a passive approach to your professional development; actively seek opportunities and take decisive steps to achieve your career goals.

7. Above all, remember this truth:

The purpose of a career is to serve your life, not the other way around. Medicine is meaningful, but it should not consume your entire identity. Let your career support your well-being and broader life goals. A successful career in medicine isn't about perfection, titles, or climbing the ladder. It's about impact, resilience, and maintaining perspective. Your work will matter, but so will your relationships, passions, and health. Keep your priorities straight, and let your career enhance your life — not overshadow it.

My final advice is a quote commonly attributed to Mark Twain: "Find a job you enjoy doing, and you will never have to work a day in your life."

The Blurred Lines of a Physician's Life

Behind the curtain is the dedication of
a physician — not a "provider."

IN A WORLD WHERE THE LINE between personal and professional often blurs, the life of a physician offers one of the most vivid examples of overlap. This image of a physician at home on Sunday morning — papers meticulously spread across a glass table, pen in hand and highlighter nearby, absorbed in study — tells a story of relentless commitment and discipline.

This snapshot captures more than a Sunday morning routine. It reveals a fundamental truth about the medical profession: The journey of becoming — and continually evolving as — a physician never ends. For those outside the field, it might seem like the culmination of medical school, residency, and board certifications marks the finish line. But as this image illustrates, the real challenge begins once the structured framework of training gives way to the self-discipline required to keep pace with an ever-accelerating world of medical knowledge.

The Lifelong Pursuit of Knowledge

The American College of Graduate Medical Education (ACGME) estimates that medical knowledge doubles every two to three years. For physicians, this means that the process of learning is lifelong. It's not driven by exams or professional milestones but by a deeper commitment: to serve patients with the best care possible. The practice of medicine demands not only mastery but humility — the recognition that there is always more to learn.

In this moment, captured at home, the physician isn't preparing for a lecture or a test. He's studying for his patients. He's reviewing the latest evidence, refining his understanding, and ensuring that he's ready to meet the next challenge that walks through his office or the operating room door. This quiet dedication is the essence of what it means to honor the Hippocratic Oath, to place patients first, and to remain ever-curious and ever-committed to the art and science of healing.

The Hidden Labor Behind the White Coat

The tools of his trade — papers, notecards, and highlighters — speak to habits honed over decades. These rituals reflect not just a love of learning but an acknowledgment of the responsibility borne by every physician. Whether it's a patient seeking answers for a persistent ailment or a family hoping for a miracle, the physician's preparedness can make all the difference.

This glimpse behind the curtain also offers a reminder to patients. The 15-minute appointment slot might be all the time spent together face-to-face, but behind those few minutes lie hours of preparation, study, and reflection. Each decision made in the exam room or operating theater is backed by a lifetime of discipline, a mountain of accumulated knowledge, and the quiet sacrifices that define the physician's calling.

The Quiet Sacrifices of a Calling

The balance is delicate. Before Sunday morning rest, before attending a religious service, before family time, and before personal pursuits comes the patient. It's a commitment that many take for granted, but one that shapes the lives of physicians and their families. It's also a calling that inspires pride and admiration in those who witness it — spouses, children, and colleagues alike.

This photograph is more than a testament to one physician's dedication; it is a celebration of a profession that demands so much yet gives even more — and sometimes so little. Beneath the quiet strength and discipline lies the reality of a profession that is, at times, strained to its limits. Diminishing Medicare reimbursements, rising administrative burdens, and the emotional toll of caring for the sick and dying all weigh heavily on the shoulders of those who have dedicated their lives to medicine.

Resilience in the Face of Adversity

Physicians are not immune to burnout, depression, or self-doubt ("impostor syndrome"). They are human, too, carrying the burden of their patients' pain while wading through the shifting tides of a healthcare system that often prioritizes financial margins over the human connection at the heart of medicine. The joy of seeing a patient recover, of solving a diagnostic puzzle, or of easing suffering is increasingly tempered by frustrations over bureaucracy and the erosion of autonomy in clinical practice.

Yet, the work continues. Why? Because for most physicians, medicine is not just a job; it is a calling (refer to essay 27). It is a profound privilege to bear witness to the most vulnerable moments in a person's life, to serve as both healer and confidant. That sense of purpose drives the late-night reading, the early-morning chart reviews, and the perpetual pursuit of knowledge. It fuels the resolve to stay current, even when the system itself feels broken.

A Personal Price for a Higher Purpose

But there's another side to this story — a side rarely acknowledged. Physicians pay a personal price for this dedication. Family time is sacrificed, hobbies are postponed, and self-care is often neglected. Partners, like the spouse who captured this photograph, bear witness to these sacrifices. They see the sleepless nights, the missed family dinners, and the quiet moments of doubt that follow a tough case or a difficult decision. They also see the unwavering commitment to something greater than oneself, a commitment that inspires both pride and heartbreak.

And yet, despite the challenges, physicians persevere. They find joy in the small victories: a thank-you note from a patient, a life saved against all odds, a moment of connection that reminds them why they chose this path in the first place. They lean on their families, their colleagues, and their communities to navigate the emotional struggles that come with the territory.

Beyond the Label of "Provider"

For the rest of us, it's a call to gratitude. To remember that the person sitting across from us in the exam room is not just a "provider" but a physician — someone who has spent countless hours in training and beyond to be there for us in our moments of need. Someone who is, even on a quiet Sunday morning, working tirelessly to stay ready, stay informed, and stay committed to the art of medicine.

Physicians are not "providers," not commodities in the cog of a vast healthcare machine, and certainly not interchangeable widgets designed to fulfill quotas or meet productivity benchmarks. The term "provider" flattens and insults the immeasurable relationship between doctor and patient, reducing years of expertise, empathy, and sacrifice into a sterile, transactional label. Medicine, at its core, is not about transactions; it is about trust.

Restoring Humanity in Medicine

The doctor-patient relationship is not a service transaction; it is a human connection. It is built on the physician's ability to see their patients as whole people, not just symptoms or diagnoses. And in turn, it depends on society's willingness to see physicians as more than just the sum of their credentials or the hours they log. It requires acknowledging their humanity — their struggles, their dedication, and their unshakable sense of purpose.

As patients, families, and communities, we must resist this commodification of care. We must honor the unique role that physicians play in our lives and in our society. And we must recognize that their dedication — captured so vividly in this photograph — is not just a reflection of their character but a reminder of what medicine truly is: a deeply human endeavor carried out by individuals who have chosen to devote themselves honorably and proudly to the service of others — and to be worthy to make that sacrifice.

Lessons from Santa for Doctors in the Modern Age

Rethink the definition of "success"
and apply it to your practice.

IMAGINE THIS: SANTA CLAUS WALKS into a modern job interview. When human resources (HR) inquires about his work schedule, Santa explains that he works one day a year. HR, unimpressed, dismisses him, stating they're seeking someone who is "always on."

The next question focuses on how he measures success. Santa replies that his mission is to spread joy and happiness, but HR counters that they are looking for measurable key performance indicators (KPIs) like revenue growth or engagement metrics.

Santa then describes his delivery system: a reindeer-powered sleigh. HR criticizes it for lacking AI or automation, deeming it unscalable. When asked where he sees himself in five years, Santa confidently states that he'll still be doing the same thing. HR flags this as a lack of leadership ambition and vision for growth.

Finally, the conversation shifts to data privacy. When Santa admits, "I know when you're sleeping. I know when you're awake," HR immediately highlights the need to discuss HIPAA compliance with the legal department.

Santa's old-fashioned ways might delight the world, but in this interview, his timeless charm doesn't quite align with the modern workplace's expectations. Yet, he has achieved unparalleled success. He has built a global brand synonymous with joy, mastered his niche, and maintained cultural relevance for centuries. What can we learn from him? Especially as doctors, immersed in a system increasingly driven by metrics and technology, how do we redefine success in medicine?

The Problem with Modern Metrics

In today's medical world, success is often reduced to numbers:

patient satisfaction scores, relative value units (RVUs), adherence to clinical guidelines, and reduced hospital readmissions. While these metrics are important, they don't tell the full story. They miss the magic — the intangible connection between doctor and patient, the moments of trust, and the joy of healing. Here are several takeaways from Santa's unconventional success story that doctors can apply to their own practice.

Building a Personal Brand

Santa's red suit, jolly demeanor, and gift-giving ethos make him instantly recognizable. In medicine, a personal brand doesn't mean flashy marketing; it's about the qualities that define your approach to care. Are you an empathetic listener? A problem-solver? An advocate for the underserved? Reflect on what you want patients and colleagues to say about you. Share your expertise through writing, speaking, or mentoring. Uphold consistency in how you approach patient care — your "red suit."

Mastering Your Niche

Santa delivers joy. He's not trying to dominate other markets — no tooth fairies or Easter bunnies in his portfolio. Similarly, doctors often feel pressured to be everything: clinician, researcher, administrator, and innovator. Academic medical centers insist on it. But true success often comes from finding and mastering your niche. Identify the areas of medicine you're most passionate about. Pursue additional training or certifications to deepen your expertise. Advocate for your niche within your institution to ensure it is valued.

Valuing the Intangible

Santa's success isn't measured by metrics but by the smiles he brings. In medicine, the intangible impacts — a patient's relief, a family's gratitude, or a life prolonged — often go unnoticed in spreadsheets. Yet, these are the moments that define why most doctors chose this path. Keep a journal of patient interactions that remind you of your purpose. Advocate for narrative medicine and storytelling in your practice. Celebrate the small victories that can't be quantified but mean everything.

Blending Tradition with Innovation

Now, imagine if Santa adapted to modern standards. He might use drones instead of reindeer for scalable delivery, replace handwritten letters with AI-generated wish analysis, and focus on market share instead of joy. Would he still be Santa? Likely not. Similarly, if doctors focus solely on metrics, they risk losing the essence of medicine.

But what if we adapted strategically, blending tradition with innovation? For instance, doctors could use AI to capture the patient narrative during office visits — details often forgotten but important to treatment planning. They could deploy telemedicine without losing personal connection and advocate for systems that prioritize quality of care over quantity.

Redefining Success in Medicine

The corporate world's definition of success — efficiency, scalability, productivity, and measurable outcomes — has its place. But as doctors, we must hold on to a broader definition that values humanity, connection, and the art of healing. There's something timeless about staying true to your unique style, just like Santa does. And like Santa, our legacy isn't just in what we do but in how we make people feel.

So, let's take a page from Santa's playbook. Let's embrace the joy, magic, and meaning in our work — and redefine success in medicine on our terms.

Recognizing Red Flags in Job Interviews

*Apart from any obvious warning
signs, trust your gut instincts.*

RECOGNIZING RED FLAGS DURING A job interview is crucial for physicians traveling along a career pathway. These subtle warning signs can reveal much about a workplace's culture and priorities, helping you avoid stepping into an environment that doesn't align with your values or long-term goals.

While preparation and thoughtful questions are essential, paying attention to your instincts can often uncover subtle indicators of potential challenges. By staying alert to these signs, you can make more informed decisions and build a career founded on growth, respect, and alignment with your principles.

An Unclear Position
One of the most glaring red flags is a lack of clarity about the role. If the interviewer struggles to articulate your responsibilities or expectations, it may signal organizational disarray or a poorly defined position. Or the interviewer may not be familiar with the medical nuances of the job. In either case, "beware" is stamped all over it.

High Turnover
High turnover in the role is another concern, as it often points to a host of issues, such as unrealistic demands, inadequate support, or poor management. If you encounter vague or evasive responses when you ask about the turnover rate, it's worth probing deeper or considering other opportunities.

No Room for Growth
Growth opportunities should be non-negotiable aspects of any role. If an employer cannot clearly outline paths for advancement or professional development, it may indicate that the position lacks the potential to support your aspirations.

For example, if you are interested in a non-clinical career (see the Afterword), utilization review positions are a dime a dozen in the health insurance industry, but where will you go once you've outgrown the position? The opportunities quickly narrow. On the other hand, pathways in the pharmaceutical industry are virtually limitless for physicians, ranging from R&D, medical affairs, and pharmacovigilance, to field positions.

Lack of Transparency
Avoid roles where discussions about compensation and benefits are dodged or downplayed. Transparency in these areas reflects the organization's commitment to fairness and respect. It's essential not to settle for vague promises or roles emphasizing long hours without tangible rewards.

An Unhealthy Culture
The company culture is another vital aspect to evaluate. Employers who describe their team as "like a family" or emphasize "wearing many hats" may unwittingly be warning you about unprofessional environments, favoritism, and excessive workloads.

"Like a family" often translates to blurred boundaries, subjective treatment, and an uneven application of rules. Similarly, "wearing many hats" typically indicates insufficient support, unclear roles, and high-pressure demands to perform tasks outside one's expertise. These situations often reflect a chaotic culture that can lead to burnout.

A Drab Interviewer
Pay attention to the tone and demeanor of the interviewer. A lack of enthusiasm or engagement can be a subtle but telling indicator of dissatisfaction within the workplace. Disinterest or distraction during the interview might suggest that the organization's culture is unmotivating or strained.

Additionally, remember that every interview is a two-way street. Interviewers who do not encourage or entertain questions from physicians may signal a lack of openness or respect for input, which could reflect broader organizational issues. If interviewers sidestep questions about team dynamics, supervisory style, or workplace values, it may signal deeper issues within the organization. Evasive answers often reflect a lack of priority on collaboration, support, or alignment with shared goals.

Lack of Onboarding

Another significant warning sign is the absence of proper training or onboarding. Even experienced physicians need time to adapt to new systems, processes, and team structures. Employers who emphasize the need to "hit the ground running" without offering adequate support set their hires up for failure. Similarly, expectations for immediate results without appropriate resources or guidance highlight a lack of foresight and a disregard for employee well-being.

The Whole Picture

Subtle cues can provide valuable insights. For instance, if a company avoids defining its work culture or responds vaguely to questions about inclusivity, teamwork, or values, it's worth questioning whether those areas are genuinely prioritized. Furthermore, a workplace that fails to foster a welcoming and inclusive atmosphere can make you feel undervalued or marginalized. An inclusive environment where diversity is celebrated and all voices are heard is essential for professional satisfaction and growth.

Trust your instincts. If something feels off during the interview — whether it's unprofessional behavior, a lack of preparation, or inconsistencies in responses — take it seriously. A haphazard process, such as changing interview platforms at the last minute or failing to read your CV beforehand, can indicate larger organizational inefficiencies. Reflecting on these signals and taking the time to ask the right questions can save significant headaches down the road.

By recognizing these red flags, physicians can avoid unhealthy work environments and make informed career choices. Beyond what's stated outright, gauge how things are said and consider the underlying message. A fulfilling career in medicine isn't just about the work you do — it's about the environment in which you do it. Ensuring that the environment aligns with your values, supports your growth, and honors respect is the foundation for long-term success.

The Hidden Snares of Medical Careers

Avoid — and break free of — career traps in medicine.

MEDICINE, AS A CAREER, IS often romanticized as a noble, unassailable path to purpose and fulfillment. Yet, even the most dedicated physicians encounter career traps — hidden pitfalls that can derail their growth, satisfaction, and impact. These traps often emerge as polished cages, camouflaged by the veneer of stability or prestige. By recognizing these hazards, physicians can chart a path that aligns with their values and aspirations while avoiding regret.

The "Someday" Syndrome

Many physicians dream of exploring new opportunities or making impactful changes but tell themselves, "Someday, I'll get to it." This mindset often leads to inertia, with "someday" becoming synonymous with "never." Progress requires action, not simply intentions. By setting small, achievable goals and building momentum, physicians can transform aspirations into tangible achievements.

The Myth of Hard Work Alone

Medicine instills a work ethic that prizes diligence and long hours. Yet, the professional world often rewards results, not effort. Physicians who focus solely on hard work without communicating their contributions risk being overlooked. Success requires delivering results and ensuring that others recognize the value created.

Living Others' Dreams

Cultural expectations, family pressures, or institutional norms can lead physicians to pursue paths that do not reflect their true desires. Are you living your parent's dreams? Your partner's dreams? Society's dreams? Or your own dreams? Chasing someone else's definition of success — whether it's a high-paying subspecialty or an academic title — can result in major dissatisfaction. Physicians must periodically reassess their goals and ask, "What do I truly want for myself?"

The Trap of Golden Handcuffs

Prestigious titles and affiliations with renowned institutions can feel like achievements, but they can also bind physicians to environments that stifle growth. The allure of a brand name often overshadows the importance of meaningful work. Physicians should prioritize opportunities where they are valued and can thrive, even if it means leaving behind the glitter of prestige.

Learning Without Doing

In medicine, continuous learning is vital, but it can also become a procrastination tool. Enrolling in courses or waiting for the "right" time to pursue a dream job often delays progress. Experience is the greatest teacher. Physicians should seek opportunities to act, gaining real-world knowledge that cannot be learned in a classroom. Sometimes, three months of experience beats three years of academic study. Remember how clinical rotations breathed life into medical school didactics?

Loyalty Over Growth

Loyalty to an institution can be admirable, but it can also hinder personal and professional development. Physicians must recognize that their worth may be higher outside their current organization. Exploring new opportunities doesn't diminish loyalty; it reflects a commitment to growth and self-respect. And remember, there is no gold watch waiting for you, even after a long, tenured position.

The Comfort Zone Illusion

Stability can be deceptive. Physicians who equate comfort with progress may inadvertently stagnate. Each role should be viewed as an experiment — an opportunity to earn, learn, or pivot. When growth stalls, it's time to reconsider staying. Multiple jobs on a CV are no longer frowned upon. The most difficult path may be the best for you.

Outdated Career Advice

Career landscapes evolve, and advice that was sound decades ago may no longer apply (think: "plastics" — the career advice given to Dustin Hoffman in *The Graduate*). Physicians should seek guidance from those who have recently achieved goals that resonate with their own aspirations. Staying current with trends and challenges in the field is essential for informed decision-making.

Navigating Work Relationships

In a profession that values collaboration, physicians may assume that everyone shares their best interests. However, not all colleagues will act as allies. Approaching relationships with professionalism and authenticity ensures that physicians maintain integrity while avoiding unnecessary conflict or disappointment. Take note of anyone who seems bent on competing with you. Let go of any urge to join in.

The Fear of Negotiation

Many physicians feel uncomfortable advocating for themselves, mistaking ambition for ingratitude. Negotiation is a vital skill that reflects self-awareness and confidence. By understanding their worth and advocating for it, physicians can secure positions and compensation that align with their contributions and expertise. Assume you have leverage and the upper hand in almost all instances.

The Courage to Create Your Path

A mentor once told me, "Career traps are like quicksand: They look stable until you realize you're sinking."

The most insidious career traps are those that quietly destroy ambition and fulfillment. Comfort, stability, and outdated notions of success can lull physicians into complacency, leaving them with regret for opportunities not pursued. Physicians must challenge themselves to recognize when to negotiate or do an about-face and walk away.

A career in medicine is a deeply personal journey. Define what success and happiness mean for you and chase that goal. By remaining vigilant against career traps, physicians can craft paths that reflect their values, passions, and potential. True progress lies in creating a career that not only heals others but also nurtures one's own sense of purpose and joy.

There's no better career path than the one you create for yourself.

ESSAY 33

The Slow Burn: Recognizing and Countering Burnout

Burnout is prevalent, but you can't fight
an enemy unless you recognize it.

In *The Truth About Burnout: How Organizations Cause Personal Stress and What to Do About It*, Christina Maslach and her colleagues define burnout as "an erosion of the soul caused by a deterioration of one's values, dignity, spirit, and will."[1] Maslach should know as much. She is a household name for her pioneering research on occupational burnout and is the co-author of the Maslach Burnout Inventory, a tool extensively used to assess burnout levels.

The three main clusters of symptoms of burnout are:

1. **Exhaustion.** The physician's physical and emotional energy levels are extremely low and in a downward spiral. A common thought process at this point is, "I'm not sure how much longer I can keep going like this."

2. **Depersonalization.** This is signaled by cynicism, sarcasm, and the need to vent about your patients or your job. This is also known as "compassion fatigue." At this stage, you are not emotionally available for your patients, or anyone else for that matter. Your emotional energy is tapped dry.

3. **Lack of efficacy.** You begin to doubt the meaning and quality of your work and think, "What's the use? My work doesn't really serve a purpose anyway." You may worry that you will make a mistake if things don't get better soon.

A Prevalent Problem

Physician burnout has been a persistent problem within the medical field. Following a peak of 62.8% in 2021, burnout among doctors has dropped below 50% for the first time since 2020, according to a 2024 survey conducted by the AMA.[2] This change represents a significant milestone in the ongoing fight against physician burnout; however, the challenge remains. It is crucial to maintain efforts to tackle the underlying causes of burnout and provide doctors with the necessary support to succeed.

Perhaps the most important understanding from the multitude of research on burnout is that it doesn't happen overnight — it's a slow, insidious process that can take root before you even notice. For physicians, the stressful nature of the profession, relentless demands, and the emotional toll of caregiving create fertile ground for exhaustion to flourish. If you're constantly drained or struggling to summon the energy to face another day, it's time to listen to the whispers of burnout before they turn into a deafening roar.

Early Signs of Burnout: Subtle but Significant

Fatigue often starts as a quiet companion, a persistent weight that eventually erodes your focus and drive. Tasks that once felt meaningful may now seem pointless, each one an uphill climb. You may find yourself procrastinating, forgetting details, or struggling to concentrate. The emotional numbness sets in next, leaving you disconnected from both your patients and your passions. Physical symptoms like unexplained headaches or muscle tension may appear, signaling that your mind and body are under siege.

Recognizing these early signs is critical. Burnout whispers before it shouts, and spotting these subtle clues can protect your energy and rekindle your passion for medicine.

The Paradox of Burnout

One of the greatest paradoxes of burnout is that we often push harder precisely when we need to pause. In the culture of medicine, where dedication is equated with long hours and self-sacrifice, resting can feel like a betrayal of your calling. Yet this relentless hustle, glorified in many professional circles, is what extinguishes the very flame that drives us.

Burnout isn't just about fatigue; it's a boundary issue. Physicians are conditioned to say yes — to their patients, their colleagues, and their institutions — often at the expense of their own well-being. The result is a cycle of overcommitment and depletion.

Systemic and Personal Factors

While burnout is often framed as a personal failing, its roots are largely systemic. Healthcare institutions, with their increasing demands and administrative burdens, often fail to provide the resources and support necessary for physicians to thrive. The lack of work-life balance, compounded by the ever-present intrusion of technology, exacerbates the feeling of being always on call.

At the same time, many physicians hold themselves to impossibly high standards. The drive to be perfect, to save every patient, and to shoulder every burden can lead to mental and physical collapse.

Reclaiming Control and Purpose

Physicians need to take many actions to counter burnout. Start with small, intentional steps. Revisit the "why" behind your work to reconnect with your purpose. Schedule short breaks during your day to reset your mind and body. Prioritize self-care by setting reminders for meals, hydration, and physical activity. These small acts of kindness to yourself can restore a sense of balance.

Boundary setting is also essential. Learn to say no when the demands become unreasonable (refer to essay 20). Advocate for systemic changes in your workplace that prioritize employee well-being, such as realistic workloads and accessible mental health resources.

The Power of Rest and Reflection

Rest is not a luxury; it is a necessity. Just as you would advise a patient to take time to heal, give yourself permission to pause. Reflect on what brings you joy — whether it's a hobby, time with loved ones, or quiet moments of solitude — and gradually reintroduce these activities into your life.

Reconnecting with your community can also help. Share your feelings with trusted colleagues, friends, or family members. This not only lightens your emotional load but also reminds you that you are not alone.

Moving Forward

Burnout may feel like a personal failure, but it's not. It's a signal that something needs to change — within yourself, your workplace, or both. By addressing the early signs of burnout, setting boundaries, and prioritizing rest, you can reclaim your passion and energy for the vital work you do. However, if recognized too late, in the throes of a major depression or other mental health crisis, professional intervention and treatment are usually necessary.

Remember, burnout doesn't define you. The same compassion you extend to your patients can — and should — be extended to yourself. Healing starts with listening, understanding, and taking the first small step toward change.

REFERENCES

1. Maslach C, Leiter MP. *The Truth About Burnout: How Organizations Cause Personal Stress and What to Do About It.* Jossey-Bass/Wiley; 1997.
2. Berg S. Physician Burnout Rate Drops Below 50% for First Time in 4 Years. American Medical Association. July 2, 2024. https://www.ama-assn.org/practice-management/physician-health/physician-burnout-rate-drops-below-50-first-time-4-years.

Physician Turnover and the Art of Leaving Well

Always exit your job in a professional manner.

PHYSICIAN TURNOVER IS AN ENDEMIC issue in healthcare organizations, impacting everything from patient continuity to institutional morale. According to recent studies, annual turnover rates among physicians hover between 5% and 10%, with a cost of as much as $1 million per departure for recruiting a replacement and sustaining losses while building a new practice.[1,2]

Early-career doctors and those in high-stress specialties are especially likely to leave, but any doctor may bolt at any stage of their career. The reasons are multifaceted, ranging from burnout and dissatisfaction with leadership to the allure of better opportunities or a desire for work-life balance. Addressing this phenomenon requires understanding not only why physicians leave but also how they exit — a process that can either bolster or damage their professional legacies.

At the heart of turnover lies the human dimension. Medicine is inherently relational, and departures disrupt more than schedules — they sever connections between doctors, patients, and colleagues. Yet, how a physician manages their exit can significantly soften the impact of these disruptions. Poorly handled departures can leave lasting scars, damaging reputations and harming the trust that underpins healthcare teams.

Conversely, leaving thoughtfully can preserve relationships, maintain professional integrity, and even pave the way for future opportunities. I left an organization on good terms after it eliminated my position (my impulse was to cause a ruckus); 13 years later, I was rehired.

Pitfalls to Avoid When Exiting

There are several common pitfalls physicians should avoid when exiting a role, each fraught with potential consequences.

First, burning bridges through dramatic or combative exits undermines years of relationship-building. While this is generally true, there are exceptions. In cases of toxic or hostile workplaces — as described in essays 41 and 42 — where the environment poses risks to mental and physical health, burning a bridge may be an act of self-preservation, setting necessary boundaries to safeguard well-being. Leaving on good terms is ideal, but it should never come at the cost of enduring harm. Walking away from a "hellscape" workplace can be the healthiest decision a physician makes.

Similarly, slacking off during the final weeks might be tempting after submitting a resignation, but doing so risks leaving colleagues overwhelmed and patients underserved. Demonstrating integrity until the very end reflects well on a departing physician's character. However, this expectation is predicated on a reciprocal relationship — if an employer fails to uphold their end of the bargain, expectations should be adjusted accordingly. Employees should not feel obligated to overextend themselves for an organization that has shown disregard for their well-being or contributions.

Equally damaging is the sudden "resignation bomb." Healthcare organizations rely on careful workforce planning, and abrupt exits can create operational chaos. Communicating intentions early and providing sufficient notice allows time for a smooth transition.

That said, the standard two-week notice is often viewed through a lens of fairness, yet many companies do not extend similar courtesies during layoffs. Employees do not owe this notice in all circumstances — contracts with physicians' employers usually dictate the terms — particularly when faced with an organization that has demonstrated little regard for its employees' welfare and futures.

Physicians should also avoid venting frustrations or bashing the organization on their way out. While it may feel cathartic, such behavior can tarnish reputations. Still, for some, the decision to withhold constructive feedback stems from the realization that the organization has already had ample opportunities to address outstanding issues.

Offering feedback may feel like wasted energy when the company has shown little interest in meaningful change. A polite and quiet departure may be the most strategic approach, maintaining professionalism without engaging in fruitless efforts.

Another critical mistake is neglecting proper patient handovers. A haphazard approach leaves colleagues scrambling to pick up the pieces and compromises patient care. Taking the time to prepare detailed handover notes demonstrates professionalism and respect for both patients and peers. However, succession planning — a once-standard practice in many organizations — has largely fallen by the wayside. This underscores the need for departing physicians to focus on personal and professional growth, even when institutional support is lacking.

Perhaps the most overlooked aspect of physician turnover is the realization that an exit is not merely an end; it is part of a professional legacy. Medicine is a small world, and paths often cross again. Maintaining connections, even after leaving, can lead to mentorship opportunities, collaborative projects, or future roles. Leaving well isn't just about professionalism — it's about safeguarding one's reputation and ensuring that the impact made within an organization endures.

Leaving with Personal Agency

There are many examples of exits that have been handled with grace and kindness. One of my colleagues returned her computer equipment with a handwritten note expressing gratitude for the opportunity to work at the organization.

This thoughtful gesture left a lasting impression, showing that even under less-than-ideal circumstances, goodwill can prevail. Such actions remind us that while entering a job often comes with excitement and hope, leaving may be tinged with disillusionment. Striking a balance between these extremes — and leaving in a manner aligned with one's values — is key.

The high prevalence of physician turnover highlights areas of concern within healthcare that demand attention. However, individual exits remain an area where personal agency can shine. By avoiding common pitfalls and embracing best practices, physicians can ensure that their departures are respectful, constructive, and forward-looking.

Those navigating toxic workplaces should feel empowered to speak out and advocate for change, knowing that silence enables harmful behaviors to persist. As the saying goes, "People may forget what you said or did, but they will never forget how you made them feel." This truth is as relevant to exits as it is to patient care, underscoring the importance of leaving with poise and integrity.

REFERENCES

1. Bond AA, Casalino LP, Tai-Seale M, Unruh MA, Zhang M, *et al.* Physician Turnover in the United States. *Ann Intern Med.* 2023;176(7). https://doi.org/10.7326/M22-2504
2. O'Connell R, Hosain F, Collucci L, Nath B, Melnick ER. Why Do Physicians Depart Their Practice? A Qualitative Study of Attribution in a Multispecialty Ambulatory Practice Network. *J Am Board Fam Med.* 2024;36(6):1050–1057. doi: 10.3122/jabfm.2023.230052R2

The Retention Remedy: Why Physicians Stay in Employed Positions

GIVEN THAT PHYSICIAN TURNOVER IS high, as discussed in the previous essay, we should be asking, "What will it take to retain them?" Physician retention has become a concerning issue, as healthcare organizations are under tremendous pressure to maintain a stable and engaged workforce.

Companies must understand that job satisfaction often hinges on intangible factors beyond compensation or perks. By exploring the key reasons why physicians leave — or stay — healthcare leaders can create environments that retain talented physicians and encourage their long-term growth and commitment.

The Evolving Landscape of Employment

The world of employment is constantly changing, and healthcare is no exception. Physicians today face a multitude of challenges, from administrative burdens to burnout, and they seek roles that align with their professional values and personal well-being. Organizations that fail to adapt risk losing skilled physicians to competitors or alternative career paths. The solution lies in recognizing what physicians truly want and delivering it consistently.

Feeling Valued and Respected

Recognition is a cornerstone of employee retention. Physicians thrive in environments where their contributions are acknowledged and celebrated. From a simple "thank you" to public recognition of achievements, acts of appreciation build loyalty. When physicians feel seen and valued, their commitment to the organization strengthens.

Careers, Not Jobs

For many physicians, career development is non-negotiable. Opportunities for growth — whether through leadership roles, academic involvement, or skill-building — keep them engaged and motivated. Healthcare organizations that invest in mentorship programs and professional development pathways demonstrate a commitment to their physicians' long-term success.

A Positive Culture

A supportive and inclusive culture leads to engagement and satisfaction. Physicians want to work in environments where collaboration, respect, and empathy prevail. Toxic work environments drive talent away, while positive cultures attract and retain top-tier physicians who are eager to contribute.

Competitive Compensation

Fair pay is a fundamental aspect of retention. Physicians often carry significant financial burdens from medical school debt, and competitive compensation reassures them that their work is valued. While money isn't everything, it's a necessary foundation for job satisfaction.

Flexibility and Work-Life Balance

The days of rigid schedules are over. Physicians increasingly value flexibility that allows them to balance demanding careers with personal and family responsibilities. Organizations that offer adaptable schedules, part-time options, and telemedicine roles cater to this growing expectation.

Meaningful Work

Purpose is a powerful motivator. Physicians who see their work as impactful and aligned with their values are more likely to stay. Creating opportunities for them to connect with patients and make a difference builds loyalty and deepens their commitment to the organization.

Recognition and Appreciation

Small acts of recognition have a significant impact. From celebrating milestones to offering words of encouragement, these gestures remind physicians that their efforts matter. A culture of gratitude cultivates satisfaction and loyalty (refer to essay 11).

Job Stability and Security

Job security is paramount, particularly in a system where health-care benefits are tied to employment. Physicians want reassurance that their positions are stable and that the organization values their long-term contribution. A revolving door of hires and dismissals undermines trust and drives talent away.

Beyond Perks: Leadership and Empathy

While perks like signing bonuses or onsite amenities may attract talent, they rarely retain it. Physicians stay when they feel their existence matters — when leaders demonstrate empathy, prioritize their well-being, and establish an environment of trust and collaboration. Retention requires more than superficial incentives; it demands genuine relationships and a shared sense of purpose.

The Broader Context

The lack of universal healthcare in the United States exacerbates retention issues. Physicians often remain employed not just for job satisfaction but also for essential benefits like affordable health insurance. Addressing these and other challenges, such as the rising cost of healthcare and administrative inefficiencies, is crucial for long-term retention.

Empowering Physicians to Stay

Retention is not a mystery. It is the result of thoughtful leadership, clear communication, and a culture that prioritizes people over profits. Leaders must ask themselves: Are we creating an environment where physicians want to build their careers? If not, it's time to reassess. By investing in physicians' professional and personal well-being, healthcare organizations can create workplaces that not only retain talent but also inspire them to thrive.

The Unseen Markers of High Performance

Redefining high performance means dispelling myths about impostor syndrome.

HIGH-PERFORMING PHYSICIANS ARE OFTEN MISREPRESENTED, with stereotypes perpetuating an image of infallible individuals who exude unwavering confidence and poise. However, the reality is far different. Traits like self-doubt, unconventional habits, and a constant feeling of being "behind" can be misunderstood as weaknesses. In truth, these are often signs of growth and ambition.

By examining the indicators of high performance, especially through the lens of medicine, we can shed light on why misconceptions about impostor syndrome and related feelings persist — and how they can be reframed as strengths.

The Impostor Syndrome Paradox

Impostor syndrome is a feeling of inadequacy that persists despite success, and it's common in medicine. In fact, Mayo Clinic researchers found that impostor syndrome is more prevalent in physicians than in other U.S. workers, with 1 in 4 physicians experiencing frequent or intense impostor syndrome symptoms and thoughts, such as[1]:

- When people praise me for something I've accomplished, I'm afraid I won't be able to live up to their expectations of me in the future.
- I'm afraid people who are important to me may find out that I'm not as capable as they think I am.
- I'm disappointed at times in my present accomplishments and think I should have accomplished much more.
- I often compare my ability to those around me and think they may be more intelligent than I am.

Yet, paradoxically, one of the most surprising indicators of high performance is feeling like an impostor. Far from signaling inadequacy, this feeling often reflects that physicians are pushing their limits, stepping into new roles, and challenging themselves. It's a sign of ambition, not failure. The discomfort of self-doubt can be a powerful motivator, propelling physicians to learn and grow.

Yet, the label "impostor syndrome" has taken on a negative connotation, suggesting something to be eradicated. This view is limiting and counterproductive. Instead of framing self-doubt as a flaw, we should view it as evidence of a professional's commitment to improvement. After all, the truly concerning individuals are those who never question their capabilities or decisions.

Redefining Confidence and Success

True confidence doesn't stem from loudly proclaiming expertise but from a willingness to listen and learn. High-performing physicians rarely dominate discussions. Instead, they ask questions, value diverse perspectives, and understand that wisdom often lies in collective insights. Similarly, their pursuit of success is not about perfection but about intentionality. They recognize that chasing the illusion of "flawless performance" is not only exhausting but also stifling to creativity and progress. Balancing excellence with realism — knowing when something is "good enough" to move forward — is a skill that defines sustainable success.

Breaking Free from Perfectionism

High performers often feel "behind," not because they are underachieving but because their standards continually rise faster than their accomplishments. This relentless drive can be both a blessing and a burden. While it fosters growth, it can also lead to burnout if left unchecked. For physicians, finding balance is key. Recognizing and celebrating achievements — without immediately focusing on the next challenge — can help ease the constant pressure to do more.

Equally important is resisting the pursuit of perfection, which can be paralyzing. Instead, embracing imperfection allows for greater innovation and adaptability, especially in the unpredictable world of medicine.

The Power of Unconventional Habits

Physicians who achieve the extraordinary often exhibit unconventional habits. They may work irregular hours, adopt unique routines, or approach problems in unorthodox ways. These personalized paths to productivity highlight their ability to tune out societal expectations and focus on what works for them. Innovation frequently appears chaotic to outsiders, but high performers trust their process, even if it defies convention.

The Role of Feedback and Criticism

Feedback is a cornerstone of growth for high-performing physicians. Actively seeking constructive criticism requires humility and the ability to separate ego from performance. It's a trait that accelerates learning and ensures continuous improvement. However, endorsing this culture of feedback also depends on the environment. Organizations must create spaces where vulnerability and honesty are valued, allowing individuals to reach their full potential without fear of judgment.

Calm in Chaos: A High Performer's Secret Weapon

One of the most remarkable traits of high-performing physicians is their ability to remain calm in chaos. While others may panic, they see opportunities in adversity. This composure is not about suppressing emotions but about reframing challenges as privileges. It reflects a mindset where pressure is viewed as a chance to excel rather than as a burden.

One of the "rules" in *The House of God* reminds us that in a "code," we should take our own pulse, suggesting first that maintaining self-control is crucial before taking action, as it allows physicians to think clearly and make the best decisions for their patients.[2]

Toward a New Understanding of High Performance

The medical profession must shift its perspective on what constitutes high performance. Traits like self-doubt, unconventional thinking, and a drive for continuous improvement are not weaknesses but markers of a dynamic, evolving professional. By reframing these qualities, we can challenge the perfectionism that plagues medicine and value a healthier, more inclusive definition of success.

Let's also reconsider the term "impostor syndrome." While it's important to acknowledge the feelings of inadequacy that often accompany growth, perpetuating the idea that these feelings signify a fundamental flaw can stifle potential. Instead, we should celebrate these emotions as signs of courage and progress. High performance isn't about being perfect; it's about being intentional, adaptable, and open to growth. When the medical community embraces these truths, it can unlock the full potential of its physicians and, in turn, provide better care for patients.

REFERENCES

1. Shanafelt TD, Dyrbye LN, Sinsky C, Trockel M, Makowski MS, *et al.* Impostor Phenomenon in US Physicians Relative to the US Working Population. *Mayo Clin Proc.* 2022;97(11):1981–1993. doi: 10.1016/j.mayocp.2022.06.021
2. Shem S. *The House of God.* New York, NY; Berkley;1978.

Your Title Doesn't Make You a Leader

*Leadership — medical or otherwise — is
earned through action, not titles.*

LEADERSHIP IS NOT DEFINED BY the title on a name badge, the letters after a name, or the authority conferred by a position. Titles might open doors, but they don't make a person a true leader. Leadership is earned through action, character, and the ability to inspire and empower others.

For physicians, who often hold titles that command automatic respect, true leadership must transcend formal roles and manifest in how they engage with their colleagues, teams, and patients. Here are the most important traits, in my estimation, that define effective physician leaders:

Empathy
Empathy is the pillar of meaningful connections. Physician leaders who understand and genuinely care about their team's well-being build trust and collaboration. Empathy allows leaders to see situations from others' perspectives, whether it's a stressed resident, an overworked nurse, or a struggling patient. This trait humanizes the leader, creating a supportive environment where challenges are acknowledged and addressed with compassion.

Integrity
Integrity acts as the leader's moral compass. In the medical field, where ethical dilemmas abound, a leader's commitment to honesty and fairness sets the tone for the team. Words and actions aligned with integrity inspire confidence. For example, a leader who admits to an error and takes corrective action exemplifies the transparency that promotes accountability and trust across the organization.

Humility
No one is infallible — and great leaders know that. Humility is

about acknowledging mistakes, being open to feedback, and showing a willingness to learn. For physician leaders, this means recognizing that even the most seasoned professional can't know everything. When leaders admit their limitations, they create a culture where others feel safe doing the same, resulting in collective growth.

Empowerment

Leadership is about lifting others. Empowering team members means providing them with the tools, opportunities, and encouragement to grow. For physicians, this might involve mentoring medical students, entrusting junior colleagues with meaningful responsibilities, or advocating for better resources for their teams. Empowered individuals become more confident, capable, and motivated to contribute.

Communication

Clear, effective communication is essential for aligning a team around shared goals. Physician leaders must articulate their vision, set expectations, and address concerns in a way that inspires confidence and collaboration. Listening is equally important. A leader who genuinely listens to their team's feedback creates a sense of inclusion and shared purpose.

Resilience

Leadership often requires navigating setbacks and uncertainty. Resilience enables leaders to stay composed and focused in challenging times. In healthcare, where crises are routine, a resilient leader's ability to adapt and remain optimistic reassures their team and models strength in adversity. This steadfastness inspires others to persevere and maintain their own resolve.

Vision

Visionary leaders see opportunities and solutions where others see obstacles. For physicians, having a vision might mean reimagining patient care processes, advocating for organizational change, or pioneering new approaches to medical education. A clear vision reduces uncertainty, provides direction, and motivates teams to innovate and excel.

Accountability

Accountability, as discussed in essay 8, begins at the top. Leaders who take responsibility for their actions and decisions — whether successes or failures — set a powerful example for their teams. A culture of accountability generates trust and ensures that all team members feel a shared responsibility for outcomes. For physicians, this might mean acknowledging the consequences of a misstep or championing a team member's success.

Emotional Intelligence

Effective leaders possess emotional intelligence, a blend of self-awareness, self-regulation, and social skills. This enables them to manage their emotions, understand interpersonal dynamics, and achieve a harmonious team environment by being cognizant and capable of influencing the emotions of others.

Physician leaders with high emotional intelligence can mediate conflicts, inspire confidence, and build strong relationships. Here are 12 mindful phrases an emotionally intelligent leader uses to lead with intention:

Mindful Phrase	Intention
"Help me see what I'm missing."	Openness dissolves defensiveness. Solutions emerge.
"Let's focus on what we can control today."	Simplify. Small steps lead to momentum.
"Can we pause to align on priorities?"	Take a deep breath. Calm begins with clarity.
"Let's make space for the team's ideas."	Invite input. Shared ownership strengthens connection.
"What support would help you move forward?"	Recognize needs. Empathy fosters trust.
"That's a great insight — can we refine it together?"	Collaboration breeds better solutions.
"I'm not sure — let me explore this further."	Create space to evaluate options without pressure.
"What's the simplest next step here?"	Action beats overwhelm. Progress over perfection.
"I hear your concerns — let's find common ground."	Build bridges. Connection moves teams forward.
"Let me revisit this after reflection."	Allow time to respond thoughtfully.

Mindful Phrase	Intention
"Thank you for being patient as we figure this out."	Gratitude eases tension. It's a leadership superpower.
"What does success look like for you?"	Align outcomes. Clarity inspires action.

Leading Under Pressure

It's often said that great leadership is born under pressure. Anyone can perform when things are easy, but real leadership shines in moments of difficulty. While most people react, great leaders respond. Physicians, especially, must master this skill — balancing clinical decisions, patient emotions, and team dynamics in high-stakes environments.

Responding vs. Reacting: The Leadership Mindset

In moments of pressure, the instinct to react can be overwhelming. A stressed-out physician might say, *"This is a complete disaster!"* — spreading panic and paralyzing action. Instead, a leader focuses on solutions: *"Let's determine the most critical issue to address first."* The difference between reacting and responding is intention: a reaction is immediate and emotional, while a response is measured and purposeful.

The Power of Equanimity

Great leaders possess equanimity: grace under pressure. While others crumble in chaos, they remain steady, guiding their teams through uncertainty. They don't shift blame but take ownership of situations. This sense of responsibility fuels their ability to be intentional with language and direction — maintaining clarity and confidence even in a crisis.

The Essence of Leadership

True leadership is about empowering others to rise, not simply standing at the top. It is about leading by example, demonstrating integrity and fairness, and creating an environment where every team member feels valued. As one colleague aptly put it, "A leader is a moral compass," guiding others and helping them find their path. Titles may grant authority, but only these traits inspire loyalty, trust, and meaningful change.

Physician leadership is not limited to administrative roles or formal hierarchies. Every doctor has the potential to lead in the clinic, at the bedside, and within the community. By embodying these traits, physicians can transform their titles into platforms for genuine leadership, creating a legacy of excellence and compassion in medicine.

ESSAY 38

Soft Skills Accelerate Your Career

Technical skills may get your foot in the door,
but it's your interpersonal and professional
abilities that really help you climb the ladder.

IN THE DEMANDING WORLD OF healthcare, technical expertise often takes center stage. Physicians are trained rigorously to master clinical skills, diagnostic accuracy, and procedural proficiency.

Yet, the reality is that most career success stems from soft skills and people skills. Technical skills may get you hired, but it is the mastery of soft skills that determines how far you rise in your career and how deeply you connect with your patients, colleagues, and the broader medical community.[1]

Emotional Intelligence: The Heart of Connection

Emotional intelligence (EQ), discussed in the previous essay, is arguably the most critical soft skill for physicians. As Maya Angelou famously noted, "People will forget what you said, people will forget what you did, but people will never forget how you made them feel."

For physicians, EQ is the ability to empathize with patients, appreciate complex interpersonal dynamics, and maintain self-awareness. Prioritizing kindness and connection over being "right" can transform patient encounters and foster trust.

The Art of Saying "No"

As discussed in essay 20, physicians often feel pressured to say "yes" to every request, whether it's an additional patient, a committee role, or extra responsibilities. However, every "yes" to the wrong thing is a "no" to the right thing. By mastering the art of saying "no," physicians protect their time and energy for tasks that align with their values and professional goals. This balance is not just helpful; it's essential for sustainable success.

Strategic Visibility: Letting Your Work Shine
In healthcare, brilliant work often goes unnoticed unless actively shared. Physicians who practice strategic visibility ensure that their contributions are recognized, whether by updating leaders on a project's impact or sharing key insights at team meetings. Waiting for others to notice your work rarely leads to advancement; taking the initiative does.

Continuous Learning: Staying Ahead
Medicine is a field of perpetual growth. The pace at which physicians learn directly influences their professional trajectory. Staying curious and embracing new knowledge — whether through journals, conferences, or reflective writing — keeps physicians at the forefront of their field. Don't wait for formal training to expand your expertise; seek opportunities to grow proactively.

Energy Management: The Foundation of Performance
In a profession where burnout is prevalent, managing energy is critical. Physicians must recognize and address their "energy leaks" — those small, unnoticed drains on their well-being that accumulate over time. Instead of wearing exhaustion as a badge of honor, focus on activities that replenish your energy and prioritize tasks that truly matter.

Time Management: Focus Over Busyness
"Always busy" is not a badge of honor; it's often a sign of being unfocused. Physicians must distinguish between being busy and being productive. Prioritizing high-value tasks, delegating effectively, and maintaining clear boundaries with time are key to achieving a fulfilling and efficient practice.

Openness to Criticism: Growth Through Feedback
Feedback is essential for professional development, especially in medicine. Physicians who react positively to constructive criticism are more likely to grow professionally, improve their clinical skills, and achieve better patient care outcomes. Instead of becoming defensive, view feedback as a gift. Phrases like "Tell me more about what excellence looks like here" or "Let's break this down into specific actions" turn criticism into actionable insights.

Lesser-Appreciated Soft Skills

Beyond those mentioned, growth and success require several other soft skills:

Adaptability in Uncertain Situations

New challenges emerge daily in medicine. Whether facing a novel disease outbreak or adapting to new medical technologies, great physicians remain flexible, learning and adjusting their approach as needed.

Effective Communication Across Teams

Clear and concise communication is vital in healthcare settings. Physicians who can articulate their thoughts well, actively listen, and bring together multiple disciplines secure patient safety and increase team efficiency.

Empathy and Compassion

Great physicians are not only clinically competent but also deeply empathetic. They recognize the human aspect of medicine, ensuring that patients and team members feel heard, valued, and respected.

Mentorship and Teaching

Physicians must invest not only in their own growth but also in the growth of others. Whether through formal teaching or informal mentorship, they share their knowledge and experience to shape the next generation of healthcare professionals.

Advocacy for Change

Practicing extends beyond the walls of the hospital or clinic. Some physicians step up as advocates, pushing for policy changes, improved healthcare access, and other improvements to benefit patients and providers.

Culinary Awareness

Culinary awareness is a soft skill that reflects discipline, adaptability, and cultural awareness — qualities that facilitate teamwork and communication. In professional and social settings, the ability to prepare, share, and appreciate food creates connection. The proverbial seat at the table that physicians aspire to often depends on how they conduct themselves over a business dinner (see essay 43).

The Gateway to Excellence

Soft skills are not optional extras; they are essential tools that accelerate a physician's career and deepen their impact. By mastering emotional intelligence, strategic visibility, energy management, and more, physicians unlock new levels of professional and personal fulfillment. Ignore these skills, and the journey remains average. Embrace them, and excellence becomes inevitable.

REFERENCE

1. Gibbs V. 85% of Career Success Comes from Soft Skills — Need a Crash Course? *Blinkist Magazine*. September 14, 2022. https://www.blinkist.com/magazine/posts/career-success-comes-from-soft-skills

Involve to Evolve: How Physicians Truly Learn

Create conditions for active learning rather than passive information transfer.

THE ANCIENT WISDOM OF THE Chinese philosopher Xunzi — "Tell me, and I forget. Teach me, and I remember. Involve me, and I learn" — captures the essence of effective education, especially in the complex, always-evolving world of medicine.

Physicians are not merely vessels to be filled with knowledge but practitioners who must internalize and apply it. This transformation from knowledge to capability happens most effectively through involvement, whether in medical training, patient care, or collaborative practice.

Harsh Truth: Disengagement in Medical Training

Many trainees and physicians find themselves disengaged, and the reasons often parallel issues in other professions: Their ideas are overlooked, they're micromanaged, or they're not given room to grow. This stagnation stifles both enthusiasm and innovation. Despite the rigorous nature of medical education, true learning doesn't occur in environments that prioritize control over collaboration or focus on tasks without meaning.

Empowering Physicians Through Involvement

Empowerment is the antidote to disengagement, and it begins with trust and active involvement. Eight strategies can contribute to a culture of learning and growth in medicine:

Delegate Meaningful Responsibilities
Rather than inundating trainees or colleagues with trivial tasks, assign them important responsibilities. This instills confidence and develops their ability to make critical decisions under pressure.

Encourage Open Dialogue
Create an environment where every team member, from medical students to senior physicians, feels safe to share ideas. Introverted individuals or those uncertain of their skills may especially benefit from one-on-one conversations, which can draw them out of the shadows.

Implement Ideas
Asking for feedback without acting on it is counterproductive. Implementing suggestions signals respect for their insights, fostering ownership and accountability.

Recognize Achievements
Acknowledging victories, both big and small, motivates individuals and reinforces the value of their contributions. Simple recognition can inspire greater effort and dedication.

Invest in Growth
Opportunities for learning and development, such as workshops, conferences, or research projects, empower physicians to expand their expertise and adapt to advancements in medicine.

Share Leadership Opportunities
Letting team members lead projects allows them to develop leadership skills, a critical aspect of medical practice that often goes unaddressed in training.

Share the Credit
Collaboration thrives in an atmosphere of mutual respect. Sharing credit reinforces teamwork and underscores the collective effort required in medicine. I was more than happy to give first-author credit to a senior resident even though I did the bulk of the writing on a published case report.

Adopt the "See One, Do One, Teach One" Tradition
One of the pillars of medical training, "see one, do one, teach one," epitomizes the power of involvement. Observing a procedure provides foundational understanding, performing it reinforces confidence and skill, and teaching it deepens mastery. In this cyclical process, learners become teachers, solidifying their expertise while empowering others

to grow. This model leads to a continuum of shared knowledge and ensures the sustainability of medical excellence.

The Dangers of Micromanagement

Micromanagement erodes trust and enthusiasm. Physicians and trainees alike need room to experiment, make mistakes, and learn from them. Overbearing supervision diminishes creativity and breeds resentment. Instead, leaders should act as guides, offering support while encouraging autonomy.

The Role of Hands-On Experience

True learning in medicine occurs when individuals are actively engaged in their work. Observing surgeries, shadowing senior physicians, or participating in case discussions are critical, but performing tasks independently solidifies knowledge. Involvement transforms abstract concepts into practical capabilities, bridging the gap between theory and practice.

Lessons from Parenting

The parallels between empowering physicians and raising children are striking. Helicopter parenting, like micromanagement, stifles growth. Allowing children — or trainees — to take risks and solve problems fosters independence and resilience. Just as parents must step back to let their children flourish, medical educators must trust their trainees to navigate challenges.

Building a Culture of Trust

Empowering physicians requires a foundation of trust. Without it, even the most innovative strategies fail. Leaders must cultivate an environment where mistakes are viewed as opportunities to learn, not failures to punish. Psychological safety and high standards are not mutually exclusive; together, they create a thriving, engaged medical team.

The Path to Mastery

Physicians truly learn when they are involved — when they are trusted to take on meaningful work, encouraged to contribute ideas, and given space to grow. Empowerment isn't about delegation for the sake of convenience; it's about fostering a culture of engagement, trust, and collaboration. As Xunzi's wisdom endures, so does the call to evolve the way we teach and learn in medicine. After all, involvement isn't just a method — it's the key to mastering the art of healing.

Dream Your Way to a Dream Career

*Never stop envisioning how you
want your career to unfold.*

SOMEONE ONCE TOLD ME, "IF you don't have dreams, you have nightmares." The meaning of this saying is fairly obvious: If someone lacks ambition, aspirations, or positive goals in life, they are more likely to experience negative thoughts, anxieties, and fears, which can manifest as a feeling like having "nightmares" in their waking life. Essentially, without a positive vision for the future — without hope and dreams — one is more susceptible to negative worries and anxiety.

For physicians, the journey to a fulfilling career often begins with an overwhelming maze of responsibilities, expectations, and external pressures. Yet, at the core of every great physician's journey lies a simple, undeniable truth: Real freedom begins when you commit to your own dreams.

In the chaos of medical training and practice, it's easy to lose sight of the dream that brought you here in the first place. Whether it was the aspiration to heal, the pursuit of knowledge, or the drive to make a difference, reconnecting with that initial vision is essential. Reflecting on your desires and setting clear goals makes every step forward feel intentional. It's this intentionality that allows you to shape a career that aligns with your values rather than one dictated by external expectations.

Freedom begins with taking ownership of your actions, your decisions, and your dreams. As physicians, we often feel constrained by systems and structures outside our control. But the truth is, the trajectory of our lives isn't determined by those systems; it's determined by the standards we set for ourselves. Stop blaming the world and start owning the choices you make.

Reflection has been a key practice in aligning my goals with my values, and journaling has become my secret weapon. I write about what excites me, what drains me, and what I truly want. It's through this habit of reflection that I've found clarity and purpose.

One of my favorite reminders is this legendary Mark Twain quote: "Most men die at 27; we just bury them at 72." It's a call to wake up and live — not just exist. Most adults rarely savor their days or look forward to the coming years. They feel that their best times are behind them. Eventually, they stop dreaming of a better life or chalk it off to age, declaring, "I'm getting old." No wonder the saying that "age is just a number" is heard commonly today — not only because Americans are living longer but also as a wake-up call to remain productive.

So many of us fall into this trap of thinking we are too old to dream, or we chase goals that look good on paper but don't actually resonate with what we want. Values-first decision-making is a game changer.

Setting my vision and goals — and aligning them with my purpose — hasn't been easy, but the effort has been life-changing. Journaling, envisioning my future, and aligning my actions with my dreams have unlocked a sense of control and freedom I didn't think was possible.

Living with Intentionality

Here's the truth: The freedom you want is closer than you think. It starts with a few intentional steps:

1. **Press Play on Your Life.** Dream it and chase it. Your dreams won't happen without action. Stop waiting for the perfect moment — it doesn't exist. The only way to know what's possible is to go for it and then evaluate the outcome.
2. **Assume Control.** Your life reflects your decisions, actions, and mindset. The moment you take ownership, you become unstoppable. Every outcome is a product of the standards you set.
3. **Build a Habit of Reflection.** Journaling isn't just for poets — it's how you figure out what actually lights you up. Without clarity, you're just spinning your wheels.

4. **Visualize Your Future.** A clear vision acts like a compass for decision-making. Plan your 10-year vision, three-year milestones, and 90-day goals. Your vision becomes your reality.

5. **Set Goals That Matter.** Start with your values. Most people chase goals that sound good but mean nothing. Let your values guide every decision, and you'll find yourself building a life you love.

6. **Stay Accountable.** Accountability is everything. Track your progress daily. Tools like a "Personal Board Meeting" — where you reflect on clinical and personal goals — can keep you focused and growing.

7. **Take Swift Action.** Analysis paralysis is the dream killer. As Mel Robbins advises, count down from five to take action: 5-4-3-2-1... GO! Her best-selling book, *The Let Them Theory*, helps you to focus on yourself, your goals, and what truly matters, allowing you to stop overthinking and start doing.

8. **Choose Play Over Grind.** Success without joy isn't success at all. Your career should fuel your adventures, not chain you to a desk. Balance deep work with wild exploration and epic experiences.

This framework isn't just about career success — it's about creating a life worth living. Plan in decades, act in moments, and build a career that reflects your highest aspirations. The freedom you crave isn't a distant dream; it's a series of intentional choices waiting for you to make them.

I don't recall who told me that nightmares ensue if you don't have dreams, but I do remember who wrote the smash 1980s hit song "Don't Dream It's Over": one of my favorite recording artists, Neil Finn, the frontman of Crowded House. Own your path, align your actions with your dreams, and watch as your vision transforms into reality.

Toxic Workplaces — Part 1: The Environment

Don't ignore the indicators of dysfunctional work environments and toxic jobs.

A TOXIC WORKPLACE DOESN'T JUST make your job unpleasant — it can take a toll on your peace of mind, your health, and even your identity. For physicians who are already in pressurized environments, the effects can be particularly damaging. Recognizing the warning signs is critical, as staying in such an environment can erode your passion for medicine and harm your well-being.

Recognizing the Red Flags

Dreading work every day is a significant indicator of a deeper problem. If every workday feels like a battle you'd rather avoid, it's not just a rough patch — it's a sign that something in your environment is fundamentally wrong.

Similarly, ignored boundaries, such as late-night calls, weekend emails, and the expectation of being constantly available, can erode your personal life. For physicians, the inability to disconnect can exacerbate burnout and leave them feeling perpetually on edge.

Constant drama, including gossip, cliques, and unproductive conflicts, creates an emotionally draining environment. In a medical setting, this drama hinders team cohesion and patient care. Broken communication, whether overly critical or nonexistent feedback, makes it impossible to thrive. Clear, respectful communication is essential in medicine, where collaboration is critical to patient outcomes.

Feeling undervalued is another sign of toxicity. When your efforts go unrecognized, it's easy to feel like just another cog in the machine. This lack of appreciation can be particularly demoralizing for physicians, who often go above and beyond for their patients.

Failing leadership — whether it's micromanagement, lack of vision, or an absence of support —creates chaos. Strong leadership should provide direction, resources, and encouragement, especially in healthcare, where the stakes are high. A culture that normalizes burnout sacrifices long-term well-being for short-term gains. If burnout becomes the norm and everyone around you is overworked and overwhelmed, it's a sign of systemic dysfunction.

High turnover rates are another indicator of toxic work environments (refer to essay 34). Frequent staff departures disrupt team dynamics and compromise patient care. No room for growth, marked by a lack of opportunities for learning and advancement, leaves you feeling stuck. Physicians should have access to ongoing education and career development to maintain competence and motivation.

Tolerated toxic behavior, such as bullying, favoritism, and discrimination, creates a culture of fear and resentment, undermining trust among colleagues. Declining health, including chronic stress and sleepless nights, is a common consequence of toxic environments. Regrettably, physicians are often the last to seek help for their own well-being.

Finally, losing yourself — where your confidence and passion for medicine begin to slip away — is a clear sign that the environment is taking a toll.

Non-Verbal Tactics to Shut Down Workplace Toxicity

Sometimes, addressing workplace toxicity doesn't require words — your actions and demeanor can speak volumes. Leveraging strategic silence allows you to stay quiet when provoked, keeping control and denying toxic behavior the attention it craves. Staying emotionally neutral by maintaining your composure and staying detached helps you avoid being drawn into conflict. Surrounding yourself with positivity by focusing on uplifting people and environments strengthens your resolve and shields you from negativity.

Resist the urge to defend yourself against fruitless arguments; let your actions speak louder than words. Limit physical proximity to toxic individuals to preserve your peace. Acknowledge negativity briefly, then move on without letting it derail your focus. Keep personal matters private to maintain professional boundaries and avoid sharing details that could be used against you.

Avoid visible frustration by keeping your emotions in check, preventing toxic individuals from getting a reaction. Finally, let your work ethic speak for itself — consistent excellence is your best defense.

Finding a Way Forward

Toxic workplaces don't just harm your career; they can consume your mental and physical health. For physicians, whose work already demands resilience, a toxic job can lead to burnout, compassion fatigue, and even serious physical and mental health problems like anxiety and depression.

Acknowledging the problem is the first step. Recognizing that your workplace is toxic allows you to stop rationalizing persistent unhappiness or health issues. Set boundaries to push back against unreasonable demands. If leadership is unresponsive, document your concerns. Seek support from trusted colleagues, mentors, or a mental health professional to discuss your experiences and options.

If the situation doesn't improve, plan your exit. Start exploring new opportunities, as your health and happiness are worth the effort. Knowing that your job is toxic and conditions are unlikely to change, exit without negotiating or bargaining. Any response to retain you will likely amount to false promises that the situation will improve.

Conclusion

As physicians, we dedicate ourselves to caring for others, but we can't neglect our own well-being. Toxic workplaces are a serious threat to your peace, identity, and health. Leaving isn't easy, but staying can cost you far more. Prioritize environments that respect and support you — because a healthier workplace means a healthier you.

Toxic Workplaces — Part 2: The Managers

Toxic managers in healthcare create ripples that extend beyond the walls of medical facilities. These managers, whether or not they are physicians, display manipulative, aggressive, or dismissive behavior and create environments of distrust, low morale, and high turnover.

DESPITE THE CRITICAL ROLE OF leadership in fostering effective healthcare delivery, toxic medical managers often thrive due to systemic flaws that prioritize short-term performance over long-term stability. Addressing the behaviors and enablers of these managers is vital to safeguarding both patient outcomes and physician well-being.

The Traits and Tactics of Toxic Medical Managers

Toxic medical managers often present a paradox: To senior leadership, they appear as high performers, but to their teams, they are sources of stress and dysfunction. These individuals frequently engage in micromanagement and excessive monitoring, and they lack trust in their teams. Instead of empowering employees, they enforce rigid control, which stifles innovation and decision-making. Public criticism, coupled with consistently negative feedback, demoralizes staff and instills a culture of fear.

Adding to this toxicity is their tendency to take credit for team successes while deflecting blame for failures. Such managers prioritize their personal image over collective growth, creating an environment where staff feel undervalued and unsupported. The result is an erosion of team cohesion, where collaboration gives way to competition, and employees hesitate to take initiative.

The Organizational Cost of Toxicity

Healthcare is uniquely vulnerable to the damages inflicted by toxic management. High employee turnover disrupts continuity of care, while diminished morale and engagement lead to reduced patient satisfaction and poorer outcomes. The financial impact is staggering, with costs associated with recruitment, training, and lost productivity reaching billions annually. Beyond these measurable effects, toxic managers create long-lasting cultural damage, suppressing innovation and creating cynicism among physicians and other employees.

Systemic factors often protect these managers. Organizations may overlook their toxic behaviors in favor of short-term results, creating a culture where fear-based motivation is normalized. Senior leadership's failure to implement robust accountability systems further exacerbates the issue, enabling toxic managers to persist unchallenged.

Recognizing and Addressing Toxic Management

Organizations must first acknowledge the signs of toxic management. High turnover rates, poor employee engagement scores, and repeated complaints about specific managers are red flags that require immediate attention.

Toxic managers often manipulate perceptions, presenting themselves as indispensable while masking their detrimental impact on teams. A clear-eyed assessment, using metrics like 360-degree feedback and team performance evaluations, is essential to expose the disconnect between their image and reality.

Addressing toxic managers involves both immediate interventions and long-term strategies. Direct feedback, coupled with specific improvement plans, can provide opportunities for change. Training programs focusing on emotional intelligence, communication, and ethical leadership help mitigate toxic behaviors. However, organizations must also be prepared to make difficult decisions. When managers fail to demonstrate meaningful improvement, termination becomes necessary to protect the organization and its employees.

Building a Culture Resistant to Toxicity

Preventing toxic management begins with organizational change. Hiring processes must emphasize leadership qualities beyond technical expertise, incorporating behavioral assessments and peer evaluations. Ongoing leadership development, mentorship, and transparent feedback systems create a culture that prioritizes accountability and employee well-being. Senior leadership must model healthy behaviors, setting a standard for empathy, fairness, and collaboration.

Policies that explicitly define unacceptable behaviors, coupled with clear consequences, reinforce the organization's commitment to a healthy workplace. Proactive monitoring of team dynamics and performance metrics allows for early detection of emerging toxic patterns. By ensuring a culture of psychological safety, organizations empower employees to speak up without fear of retaliation.

When employees feel free to speak their minds, climate assessments can be requested. These systematic evaluations are designed to gather insights into the overall work environment within an organization. Climate assessments focus on understanding employees' perceptions and experiences of their workplace, including aspects such as communication, leadership effectiveness, inclusivity, and morale.

Conducted through surveys, interviews, or focus groups, climate assessments provide valuable data that can highlight strengths and areas needing improvement. By identifying patterns and trends, organizations can tailor interventions to foster a more supportive and engaging work atmosphere. Regular climate assessments help ensure that the organizational culture aligns with its values, promoting a healthy and productive environment for all employees.

The Path Forward

Toxic medical managers represent a significant threat to healthcare systems, undermining both employee well-being and patient care. Addressing this issue requires more than surface-level fixes; it demands a transformation of leadership practices and organizational culture. By prioritizing the identification, development, and accountability of leaders, healthcare institutions can create environments where both employees and patients thrive.

Ultimately, the fight against toxic management is a commitment to the values that underpin healthcare itself: compassion, integrity, and the unwavering pursuit of better outcomes for all.

Dealing with Job Rejection Requires an Open-Minded Perspective

Reframe rejection as an opportunity to network and grow professionally.

I'VE APPLIED TO MANY JOBS over my career, and I've been rejected by far more companies than I care to remember. One of my first crushing rejections was for a position as chairman of behavioral health at a university-affiliated community hospital.

I breezed through the interviews to the last stage: a formal dinner with the major stakeholders — with an invitation extended to my spouse. I was passed over for the job in favor of a more senior psychiatrist. My spouse said I shouldn't have ordered the lobster dinner. Who knows? Perhaps I should have ordered a rubber chicken instead, and they would have viewed me as more modest and relatable.

The point is, in the end, it's often the small details and perceptions that can unexpectedly influence decisions. Despite this setback, I learned valuable insights into the selection process and continued to grow professionally, eventually finding opportunities that aligned more closely with my skills and aspirations. I also learned that what you eat (and drink) says a lot about you (refer to essay 38).

Later in my career, my position at a large health insurance company was eliminated. I was given a month to get my affairs in order. In less time, I was hired by a pharmaceutical company, marking the start of a 12-year career in that industry. Who knows. If I hadn't been given my pink slip at the insurance company, I might not have been so fortunate to discover a new path that ultimately enriched my career and broadened my expertise.

This unexpected turn of events opened doors to opportunities I hadn't previously considered, allowing me to make significant contributions to the pharmaceutical field and further develop my professional skills.

Demonstrating Professionalism

Rejection is an inevitable companion in a medical professional's journey. Whether it is being denied a residency spot, a fellowship, a coveted attending position, or the prospect of joining a group practice, how one approaches rejection can shape one's career trajectory. Physicians should view rejections not as personal failures but as stepping stones toward growth. Each rejection offers an opportunity for introspection, allowing physicians to identify gaps in their experience or approach and address them with purpose.

Responding to job rejections with grace is paramount. A professional response, whether it involves thanking the organization for the opportunity or expressing interest in future positions, conveys maturity and resilience. For physicians, who are often held to high standards of communication and demeanor, such behavior reinforces their commitment to excellence. Demonstrating professionalism in the face of rejection also builds bridges for future opportunities, as recruiters and hiring committees often revisit prior applicants when new roles emerge.

Maintaining a Growth Mindset

Physicians thrive on learning from their experiences, and job rejections should be no exception. Reaching out to request feedback is an effective way to identify areas for improvement. A missed opportunity might highlight the need for additional certifications, enhanced interpersonal skills, or even a stronger narrative during interviews.

By actively seeking constructive criticism, physicians signal their willingness to grow — a trait that is as vital in professional development as it is in clinical practice. (I did reach out to the physician responsible for the hiring at the community hospital. He told me it was basically a matter of experience — not the lobster dinner.)

Networking Through Rejection

Rejections can serve as networking opportunities, especially when handled with a forward-thinking approach. By responding to rejection emails and expressing an interest in being considered for future openings, physicians keep the door ajar for potential opportunities. Each interaction, even one that ends in rejection, can expand a professional network and open pathways to roles that may align better with one's skills and aspirations.

Resilience in the Long Game

The journey to becoming a physician demands resilience, and job rejections are no different from the challenges faced in medical school or residency. It is crucial to approach rejection with a balanced perspective. Emotional reactions like bitterness or resentment can hinder future opportunities and tarnish professional reputations. Instead, physicians should focus on the long-term goal of finding positions where they can thrive and contribute meaningfully to patient care.

Building a Narrative of Perseverance

Rejection is an opportunity to refine one's narrative. I've emphasized throughout this book that physicians often function as storytellers, communicating complex medical information to patients and families. Similarly, each rejection offers a chance to reshape one's professional story, emphasizing adaptability, determination, and the ability to turn setbacks into successes. This approach is especially pertinent in narrative medicine, where the physician's journey is as much a part of the story as the patient's.

Conclusion

Job rejections are not endpoints but rather pivotal moments that invite growth, reflection, and reinvention. Physicians who approach these moments with professionalism, a willingness to learn, and a focus on future opportunities position themselves as resilient and adaptive leaders in their field. In medicine, as in life, setbacks are often the precursor to breakthroughs.

The Leadership Power of Introverted Physicians

*Physicians who exude a quiet confidence
often provide strong leadership.*

IN MEDICINE, LEADERSHIP IS OFTEN associated with extroverted traits — commanding attention, energizing teams, and thriving in the spotlight. Yet, many of the most effective physician leaders are introverts who bring focus, empathy, and thoughtful action to their roles. About 35% of physicians self-identify as introverts on the Myers-Briggs Type Indicator (MBTI), with another 38% reporting a mix of introverted and extroverted traits.[1]

Introversion is not a limitation in medicine; it is a unique strength that enables a quiet but positive influence on patient care and team dynamics. I make this statement as an introvert who has held several leadership positions and has been amply rewarded for my roles with the satisfaction of knowing that my approach has led to a collaborative, respectful environment where both colleagues and patients feel heard and valued. This recognition has affirmed that leadership in medicine is not about fitting a specific mold but about leveraging one's unique qualities to inspire and guide others effectively.

Transforming Leadership Through Language

Introverted physicians contribute to their teams through intentional, meaningful communication. They do not speak just to fill silences; instead, they weigh their words carefully. When they share their thoughts during clinical rounds or strategy meetings, their insights are important and carry significant weight. This clarity and precision ensure their contributions are not only heard but also respected.

A single phrase can escalate tension or defuse it. Here's how great leaders refine their language to inspire trust and action:

Negative Phrase	Positive Alternative
"You need to calm down."	"I'm noticing we're both getting tense. Should we take a break?"
"You should have known better."	"What can we learn from this for next time?"
"It's not my fault."	"I may have contributed to this. Help me understand where."
"Why isn't this done yet?"	"What's the most immediate blocker we need to address?"
"I already told you that."	"Here's another way to think about this."
"Just figure it out."	"What specific help do you need to move this forward?"
"That's not my problem."	"How can I help you solve this?"
"That's how we've always done it."	"Talk me through your new idea — what would improve?"

Building Trust Through Listening

Listening is the opposite side of the coin of speaking. The ability to listen deeply is a hallmark of effective physician leaders, and introverts excel in this area. Whether listening to a patient's concerns or a colleague's perspective, introverted doctors create a sense of being truly heard. This builds trust and strengthens relationships, igniting collaboration among medical teams and maximizing the therapeutic alliance with patients.

Leading by Example: Actions Over Words

Introverted physicians lead through their actions rather than grand declarations. Their calm and steady demeanor during medical crises sets an example for their teams. They inspire confidence in those around them by demonstrating resilience and unwavering focus. This quiet strength is a stabilizing force in a field where composure often translates to better outcomes for patients and teams alike.

Deep Connections: Quality Over Quantity

In the practice of medicine, meaningful relationships often have more impact than a broad network of acquaintances. Introverted leaders excel at forging deep connections with their patients, mentees, and colleagues. These strong, authentic bonds create a foundation for trust and collaboration that is vital for effective healthcare delivery and team cohesion.

The Power of Observation

Introverted physicians possess a heightened ability to observe subtleties that others might miss. A change in a patient's tone, a colleague's unspoken hesitation, or an overlooked detail in a clinical chart — these observations often lead to critical insights. This attention to detail enhances diagnostic accuracy, improves patient care, and strengthens team dynamics by addressing issues before they escalate.

Clear Communication: Straight to the Point

In medicine, where time is often a critical factor, clear and concise communication is essential. Introverted leaders are skilled at delivering messages without unnecessary complexity or embellishment. Their ability to distill complex information into actionable insights ensures their instructions are understood and implemented effectively in fast-paced clinical settings.

Solution-Oriented: Results Over Recognition

Introverted physician leaders focus on solving problems rather than seeking recognition. Their results-driven approach prioritizes patient outcomes and team success over personal accolades. This humility fosters a collaborative atmosphere and enhances trust, creating a culture where the collective mission of improving patient care takes precedence.

Setting Boundaries: Protecting Energy

The demanding nature of medicine can lead to burnout without proper boundaries. Introverted physicians are adept at recognizing their limits and prioritizing self-care. By saying "no" to unnecessary obligations and focusing their energy on what truly matters, they maintain their effectiveness and model healthy work-life balance for their teams.

Leading with Empathy

Empathy is at the heart of introverted leadership in medicine. By tuning into the emotions and needs of their patients and colleagues, introverted physicians create a supportive and understanding environment. This emotional intelligence not only improves patient satisfaction but also allows a sense of psychological safety within medical teams, encouraging open communication and collaboration.

Encouraging Others to Shine

Introverted leaders in medicine often empower others to step into the spotlight. By mentoring junior physicians, supporting colleagues, and creating opportunities for others to succeed, leaders amplify their influence without seeking personal recognition. This approach builds strong, capable teams and ensures the next generation of leaders is well-prepared to continue advancing healthcare.

The Quiet Strength of Introverted Physicians

Introversion is not a barrier to leadership in medicine; it is a distinct advantage. Introverted physicians lead with quiet confidence, empathy, and focused action. Their ability to listen deeply, communicate clearly, and build meaningful connections enhances patient care and strengthens medical teams. In a field where competence and compassion are equally important, introverted leaders make an enduring impact.

At the same time, it is crucial to recognize that leadership is not one-size-fits-all. Extroverted physicians bring their own invaluable energy, charisma, and visibility to leadership roles, creating diverse and dynamic teams. Ultimately, the best leaders in medicine are those who harness their authentic strengths to inspire and guide others, regardless of their personality type.

REFERENCE

1. Lam J. Embracing Introversion in Medicine. in-Training. April 29, 2019. https://in-training.org/embracing-introversion-in-medicine-18169#:~:text=A%20Medscape%20report%20surveying%20over%2015%2C000%20physicians,respondents%20reporting%20to%20be%20somewhere%20in%20between

Stop Sabotaging Yourself — And Your Career!

In the demanding field of medicine, where trust and respect are highly regarded, self-sabotaging behaviors can quietly erode the foundation of a successful career. Physicians are often seen as paragons of knowledge and competence, yet even the most accomplished among us can fall prey to habits that undermine our credibility and professional relationships. Recognizing and addressing these behaviors is the first step toward ensuring your career is marked by respect and fulfillment.

The Power of Self-Awareness

The journey to overcoming self-sabotage begins with awareness. Many of these behaviors are so ingrained that they operate unconsciously, yet they significantly impact our professional lives. As Carl Jung wisely noted, "Until you make the unconscious conscious, it will direct your life, and you will call it fate." By shining a light on these habits, we can begin to change them, paving the way for personal and professional growth.

Over-Apologizing: Reclaiming Your Space

In the television series *NCIS*, the character Leroy Jethro Gibbs, played by Mark Harmon, had a set of personal rules he lived by known as "Gibbs' Rules." One of those rules was: *Never apologize. It's a sign of weakness* (rule #6). This rule reflects Gibbs' tough, no-nonsense leadership style, though he occasionally breaks it when circumstances call for genuine humility. Gibbs' actions often show that he values integrity and accountability, even if he rarely verbalizes apologies.

One of the most common self-sabotaging habits is over-apologizing. While humility is a virtue, excessive apologies can project insecurity and diminish your authority. It is crucial to reserve apologies for situations where harm has been caused. By doing so, you not only preserve your credibility but also reinforce your confidence and self-respect. Recognize that your time and presence are valuable, and practice standing firm in your professional interactions.

Hailing Your Achievements

Minimizing your accomplishments might seem like humility, but it can prevent others from recognizing your true value. Physicians often downplay their successes, which can lead to being overlooked for opportunities and promotions. Instead, own your achievements and accept compliments graciously. This not only builds your self-esteem but also sets a standard for how others perceive your contributions. Celebrate your successes as a testament to your hard work and dedication.

The Pitfalls of Being a "Know-It-All"

In the medical field, knowledge is power, but acting as a "know-it-all" can alienate colleagues and stifle collaboration. It's important to remain open to new ideas and be willing to learn from others. Acknowledging that no one has all the answers reaffirms and reinforces continuous learning. By showing curiosity and humility, you increase your chances of connecting with peers and patients alike.

The Importance of Boundaries

Over-sharing personal information can blur professional boundaries and create discomfort. It is essential to be mindful of what you share and with whom, especially in a clinical setting. Establishing appropriate boundaries not only protects your personal life but also safeguards your professional image. Authentic relationships are built on trust and respect, which are nurtured through thoughtful communication and discretion.

Guarding Your Time and Energy

Being too available can lead to burnout and the perception that your time is not valuable. As a physician, it's important to set boundaries and prioritize your well-being. Understand that you cannot please everyone, and it's perfectly acceptable to say "no" (refer to essay 20). This not only protects your mental health but also allows you to focus on what truly matters in your career and personal life.

Authenticity in Professional Relationships

When writing personal narratives, it is essential to use your authentic voice. The same is true in practice. Hiding your true self prevents you from forming genuine connections with colleagues and patients. Embrace your individuality and seek out environments where you are appreciated for who you are. Authenticity creates trust and forges deeper, more meaningful relationships. By being true to yourself, you create a professional presence that is both respected and admired.

Taking Control of Your Narrative

Seeking sympathy and playing the victim can undermine your agency and professional reputation. Instead, focus on what you can control and take proactive steps to address problems. By adopting a solutions-oriented mindset, you empower yourself and those around you, building credibility as people come to appreciate your problem-solving skills.

Accepting Failure as a Learning Opportunity

Fear of failure is a powerful form of self-sabotage that can prevent us from seizing opportunities. This fear can manifest as procrastination, self-doubt, or avoidance of challenges. To overcome this, reframe failure as a natural part of the growth process. By viewing setbacks as learning opportunities, you build resilience and open yourself up to new possibilities. This shift in perspective can be transformative, enabling you to take bold steps forward in your career.

The Path to Professional Fulfillment

Self-sabotage is a complex issue rooted in subconscious patterns and past conditioning. While awareness is the first step, overcoming these habits requires intentional self-work and sometimes professional support, mentoring, and coaching. By confronting these behaviors and making conscious changes, you position yourself for greater success and credibility in your career. Embrace your potential and remember that your journey to professional fulfillment is not just about what you achieve but also about how you grow and evolve along the way.

Smart Habits for a Successful Career

*Ensure success in your career by integrating these
small yet powerful habits into your routine.*

Transforming your career and professional journey as a
physician is not about grand gestures or sweeping changes but
rather the integration of small, powerful habits into your routine.
By adopting these strategies, physicians can navigate their careers
with clarity, productivity, and growth.

Quarterly Quests Over Annual Goals

The traditional approach of setting annual goals often leads to overwhelming tasks and diluted focus, especially in the fast-paced world
of medicine. Instead, consider breaking down your objectives into
12-week cycles or Quarterly Quests.

For example, a psychiatrist might focus on three significant goals,
such as learning new patient engagement techniques, completing a
research paper, and attending a specialized workshop in EMDR (Eye
Movement Desensitization and Reprocessing). This method allows
for flexibility and adaptability, ensuring your goals remain relevant
and achievable. A focused 90-day quest keeps your objectives clear
and your motivation high, imparting a sense of accomplishment
and progress.

Weekly Productivity Review

A consistent weekly productivity review is essential for maintaining momentum and ensuring alignment with your quarterly goals.
Spend 20 minutes each week reflecting on your achievements and
challenges. For instance, you might review the number of patients
seen, the outcomes of treatment, or progress on continuing education requirements. This practice not only celebrates your successes
but also provides valuable insights into areas needing improvement.

By prioritizing your top three tasks for the upcoming week, such as preparing for a lecture, updating patient records, or learning a new medical software, you maintain a clear path forward, ensuring that your efforts remain directed and purposeful.

Daily Morning Manifesto

Begin each day with a purposeful morning manifesto (refer to essay 29). This involves reflecting on your weekly priorities and identifying the day's most critical task, such as preparing for a complex case review or consulting with a multidisciplinary team. By approaching each day as an adventure with clear intentions, you cultivate consistency. This daily ritual sets the tone for focused and intentional work, aligning your actions with your broader goals and values.

Focus Logs for Accountability

Enhancing focus through accountability can significantly impact productivity. By logging the time spent on key tasks, such as patient consultations, research, or administrative duties, you create visibility in your efforts, leading to substantial productivity gains. This practice not only tracks your progress but also highlights patterns that can be optimized for better efficiency and effectiveness.

Multimodal Multitasking

Incorporate multimodal multitasking into your routine by utilizing downtime productively. Listening to medical podcasts or audiobooks while commuting to the hospital or clinic can significantly advance your knowledge. When used wisely, these small moments contribute to your professional development without requiring additional time.

Professional Networking Rituals

Networking is a critical component of career success in medicine, and dedicating time each week to connect with industry peers on platforms like LinkedIn, Doximity, and Research Gate can be invaluable. Engaging with content, commenting thoughtfully, and strategically expanding your network can lead to collaborations on research projects, invitations to speak at conferences, or insights into new treatment methods.

Continuous Learning Commitment

Commit to learning something new each month through medical journals or online resources such as webinars. For example, a family medicine physician might explore new developments in telemedicine or advances in pharmacology. Continuous learning not only keeps you updated with the latest in your field but also empowers you with knowledge that can drive innovation and growth in your practice.

Mindful Breaks for Clarity

Incorporating short, mindful breaks into your workday can reset focus and reduce stress, which is crucial in high-pressure environments like hospitals. A refreshed mind is more productive and creative, allowing you to approach tasks with renewed energy and perspective. These breaks are a simple yet effective way to maintain overall well-being and work performance.

Feedback Loop for Improvement

Regular feedback is vital for personal and professional development. By seeking feedback on your work and development, such as patient satisfaction surveys or peer reviews, you gain valuable insights that can guide improvement. Utilize tools like LinkedIn polls or direct messages to gather input from your network, perpetuating a culture of continuous growth and adaptation.

Personal Branding Consistency

Maintaining a consistent personal brand on social media is essential for building trust and recognition in the medical community. Regularly posting content that reflects your professional values and expertise, such as articles on treatment and prevention, helps establish a strong personal brand. Consistency in messaging not only enhances your professional reputation but also solidifies your standing as a thought leader in your field.

Success in your medical career or personal development ultimately stems from daily intentionality and consistency. By integrating these smart habits into your routine, you pave the way for a successful and fulfilling professional journey.

ESSAY 47

Career Advice I Wish I Had Received Earlier

Seek career advice from trusted colleagues and mentors. Otherwise, you'll learn the hard way.

SOME OF THE BEST CAREER advice I ever received was not given to me in medical school. Nor was it told to me by my residency director or another faculty member. I read it in a book — *The Success Principle,* by Ronald Yeaple, PhD — midway through my career. How I wish someone had passed that information on to me sooner.

Here is a list of career lessons I've learned through experience — lessons that inspired many essays in this book, and that I should have been taught earlier in my career but was not:

The Importance of Connections
One of the most significant lessons I learned outside the classroom is the power of relationships. As physicians, we often focus on merit — grades, board scores, and clinical skills — but the truth is that who you know can be just as important as what you know.

After I was roundly rejected from every medical school the first time I applied, I summoned the courage to call one of the doctors who interviewed me. To my surprise, he remembered me and said he was impressed with my application. He invited me to his home for coffee on a Saturday morning. He told me to try to improve my grades and MCATs during my gap year, and if I was successful, he would re-present my application to the admission committee. It worked, and I was accepted.

Building connections with colleagues, mentors, and even patients can open doors that might otherwise remain closed. During residency, I witnessed a fellow physician secure a prestigious fellowship not solely because of her academic excellence but because she had nurtured a strong relationship with a mentor who advocated for her. This experience taught me that networking is not just a side task but a vital component of career development.

169

Accepting the Role of Feedback

Feedback, especially in the medical field, is often perceived with trepidation. However, accepting constructive criticism is essential for growth. Early in my career, I struggled with feedback, viewing it as a personal affront rather than a tool for improvement.

It wasn't until a senior colleague advised me to view feedback as a gift that I began to see its true value. By actively seeking feedback and using it to refine my practice, I noticed a marked improvement in my clinical skills and patient interactions. This shift in mindset allowed me to progress more rapidly and effectively in my career.

Managing Career Transitions

It's also crucial to recognize when you've outgrown a position. As physicians, we often tie our identities to our roles, making it difficult to acknowledge when a job no longer aligns with our career goals or personal values.

I once remained in a role long after it had ceased to challenge or fulfill me, fearing that leaving would be seen as a failure. Eventually, I realized that outgrowing a job is not a setback but a natural part of professional evolution. Moving on to a new position that better aligned with my aspirations reinvigorated my passion for medicine and opened new avenues for growth.

The Myth of Perfection

Perfectionism is a common trait among physicians, driven by the high risks of our work. However, striving for perfection can lead to burnout and hinder progress. I learned the hard way that aiming for progress rather than perfection is more sustainable and rewarding. By setting realistic goals and celebrating incremental improvements, I was able to reduce stress and maintain a healthier work-life balance. This approach improved my well-being and also added to my skills as a physician.

The Power of Soft Skills

As discussed in essay 38, soft skills are vital to career success. While technical skills are fundamental, soft skills such as empathy, adaptability, and communication are equally crucial. These attributes can distinguish a good physician from a great one.

Early in my career, I focused heavily on honing my writing skills for medical journals, spending much time in my office and overlooking the importance of communication and teamwork. Two faculty members informed the chairperson of the psychiatry department that I was "nowhere to be found." It almost cost me my job. I realized that academic prowess alone was insufficient to get by. Soft skills play a critical role in interpersonal relationships and should not be taken lightly.

Advocating for Yourself and Your Team

Negotiation is another skill that is often underestimated. As physicians, we are taught to advocate for our patients, but we must also learn to advocate for ourselves and our teams. Whether negotiating a salary, a work schedule, or resources for your team, standing up for yourself is crucial.

I learned this lesson when I successfully negotiated additional support for a book I was writing while working for a health insurance company, arguing that the publicity it would generate would be good for the organization as well. Advocacy is not just about self-interest; it's about ensuring that you and your team have what you need to succeed.

Prioritizing Well-Being

Finally, prioritizing your well-being is paramount (see essay 52). The demands of the medical profession can easily lead to burnout if self-care is neglected. I've seen colleagues sacrifice their health for their jobs, only to realize too late that no position is worth such a cost. By prioritizing my health, I've been able to sustain my career and passion for medicine.

While these lessons are not taught in medical school, they are integral to a fulfilling and successful career.

How to Give Feedback to Your Boss (Without Getting Fired)

PROVIDING FEEDBACK TO YOUR BOSS is like walking through a minefield — one misstep and it could backfire, leading to tension, mistrust, or professional repercussions. Many physicians hesitate to voice concerns, fearing retaliation or jeopardizing relationships with leadership. However, when done correctly, providing feedback up the chain of command can lead to improved patient care, stronger leadership, and a more cohesive clinical team. The key lies in delivering feedback with tact, clarity, and a focus on solutions. Here's how to do it right.

Timing Is Everything

Choosing the right moment to offer feedback is critical. Attempting to share concerns during a high-stress situation — such as rounds, a busy clinic, or mid-crisis in the ER — can make your boss defensive, reducing the chances of a productive conversation. Instead, wait for a calmer moment and request a private discussion.

A good strategy is to start with a positive comment before addressing your concern. For example, "I appreciate how you've been advocating for the team's needs. I had a thought on how we might improve communication about schedule changes to avoid last-minute disruption." This approach sets a constructive tone and ensures your feedback is received in the right spirit.

Lead with Solutions

Complaints without actionable suggestions can come across as mere grievances rather than useful insights. Instead of stating, "We're always short-staffed in the ICU," reframe it as, "Would it be possible to reevaluate shift coverage to ensure better patient care and physician well-being?" This shifts the conversation from a problem to a collaborative solution, making it easier for your boss to engage without feeling criticized.

Be Clear, Not Cryptic

Vague feedback leads to misunderstandings and inaction. Instead of saying, "Communication could be better," specify the issue and propose a fix: "Not getting timely updates on policy changes makes it difficult to adjust workflows. Could we implement a standardized update via email or our EHR system?" Specific examples reinforce your point and provide a clear path for improvement.

Use "I" Instead of "You"

Framing feedback with "I" statements instead of "You" statements prevents defensiveness and keeps the conversation constructive. Rather than saying, "You don't give enough autonomy," say, "I feel that more decision-making flexibility would allow me to optimize patient care. Is there a way to balance oversight with clinical independence?" This keeps the focus on your perspective and invites dialogue rather than conflict.

Rehearse if You're Shy

To effectively manage up, a physician, especially one who is shy, should prepare thoroughly by clearly defining the issues they want to address and the desired outcomes. Use data or specific examples to support your case, and practice concise, assertive communication. If direct confrontation feels daunting, start with a written communication or rehearse with a trusted colleague to build confidence. There's always a good chance your boss will think *less* of you for not broaching a troubling situation, which could reinforce an abusive pattern of behavior.

Physician vs. Non-Physician Boss: Does It Matter?

A significant factor in giving feedback effectively is understanding whether your boss is a physician or a non-physician administrator. Physician leaders often have firsthand experience with the challenges of clinical work and may be more receptive to concerns about patient load, burnout, or medical decision-making autonomy. In contrast, non-physician administrators may focus more on financial efficiency, regulatory compliance, or institutional priorities.

Grounding feedback in clinical realities and patient outcomes can be particularly effective when dealing with a physician boss. When addressing a non-physician leader, framing concerns in terms of workflow efficiency, patient satisfaction, and institutional goals may lead to better receptivity. Adjusting your approach based on your boss's background and personality can increase the likelihood of your feedback leading to meaningful change.

Know When to Let It Go
Not every issue is worth addressing. Choose your battles carefully, as the saying goes. Before giving feedback, ask yourself: "Does this impact patient care, physician well-being, or team efficiency?" If the answer is no, it may not be worth the discussion. Save your energy for issues that align with broader institutional goals that have the potential to resonate fully.

End with a Vision
Effective feedback doesn't just highlight problems — it paints a picture of a better future. Ending on a visionary note ensures your boss sees the long-term benefits of your suggestions. Try something like, "If we implement this change, I believe it could streamline our workflow and improve patient care and staff morale." Vision-driven feedback inspires action and positions you as a team player committed to excellence in healthcare.

Managing Up: The Bigger Picture
Beyond individual feedback conversations, long-term success in providing input to leadership involves mastering the art of "managing up." This means understanding your boss's leadership style, aligning with institutional goals, and fostering a relationship built on trust and reliability. Soft skills such as emotional intelligence, active listening, and adaptability are invaluable in this process.

If trust erodes in your relationship with a boss, diagnosing the root cause and addressing it quickly is essential. Conflict is inevitable in any workplace, but handling it professionally can turn challenges into growth opportunities. When conflicts persist, seeking guidance from a mentor or a physician leadership coach can provide strategies to manage difficult dynamics without jeopardizing your career.

Knowing When to Move On

Sometimes, despite your best efforts, the workplace environment remains toxic or unresponsive to constructive feedback (refer to essays 41 and 42). If your professional growth is stunted, your feedback is consistently ignored, or your work environment becomes intolerable, it may be time to consider new opportunities. A successful medical career isn't just about surviving in one institution — it's about thriving in an environment where your expertise and contributions are valued.

Final Takeaway

Giving feedback to a boss — whether a fellow physician or an administrator — isn't about proving you're right; it's about enabling progress. By approaching the conversation with the right timing, constructive framing, and a vision for improvement, you can transform feedback from a workplace risk into a powerful tool for positive change. Mastering these skills will not only make you a valuable team member but also help you build a career grounded in effective communication and leadership.

ESSAY 49

Recognize the Warning Signs of Impending Job Termination

Learn to read the tea leaves and foresee winds of change.

IN TODAY'S DYNAMIC HEALTHCARE ENVIRONMENT, physicians face job insecurity similar to that of other employees, and perhaps more so. Several factors correlate with physicians being fired. These include being the first person in a new or unclear job, working for an entity with sustained financial losses, and persistent conflict with a boss or board member concerning personal style or organizational strategy. Additional variables include recent termination or departure of a boss, recent merger or acquisition, and widespread organizational downsizing or re-engineering.

Recognizing these early warning signs of potential termination can empower physicians to make decisions about their careers before the axe falls. Understanding these signals can help soften the blow of job loss and facilitate a smoother transition to new opportunities.

Behavioral Changes from Management
One of the first indicators of job insecurity is a shift in management's behavior. Reduced communication, where your manager avoids engaging in meaningful conversations, can signal a breakdown in the professional relationship. Exclusion from meetings or projects may indicate a diminishing role within the organization. Increased micromanagement often reflects a lack of trust in your abilities, while frequent negative feedback and unclear expectations can undermine your confidence and performance.

These behavioral changes suggest a need for open dialogue with your boss or someone in management to address any concerns and clarify expectations rather than retreat or disengage.

Shifts in Your Workload
Changes in your workload can also be telling. A lack of new assignments or the removal of responsibilities may indicate that your

176

contributions are no longer valued. Unusually negative performance reviews, especially when they seem unwarranted, can be a precursor to termination. These shifts should prompt self-reflection and a discussion with your supervisor to understand the underlying reasons and explore ways to improve.

Company-Wide or Organizational Changes

Sometimes, the signs are not personal but rather a reflection of broader organizational changes. Budget cuts, a hiring freeze, or a perceived reduction in the importance of your role can all impact job security. These changes may not be within your control, but being aware of them can help you prepare for potential outcomes.

I've had to deal with *MADness* — mergers, acquisitions, and downsizing — numerous times. Security is never guaranteed in these circumstances, but it's better to be on the acquiring end than the acquired. Regardless, mergers rarely have a human side, as business imperatives drive these transactions.

Social and Professional Dynamics

The workplace atmosphere can also offer clues. If colleagues begin to act differently, seeming hesitant to engage, it could be indicative of rumors or known changes about your employment status. A loss of privileges without explanation or circulating rumors about layoffs can further contribute to a sense of instability. Maintaining strong professional relationships and open communication can help circumvent these social dynamics.

Direct Indicators

More direct indicators of impending termination include being placed on a Performance Improvement Plan (PIP) or being assigned tasks that are difficult or impossible to achieve. If your boss avoids discussing your future within the organization, it may be time to consider your options. These direct signals require careful evaluation of your position and proactive steps to secure your career.

Strategic Response

If you notice several of these signs, acting strategically rather than reacting impulsively is crucial. Resigning immediately to "save face" can have significant financial implications, including the loss of severance or unemployment benefits. Instead, consider updating your resume, networking with colleagues, and exploring new opportunities while still employed. Open communication with management about your role and performance can sometimes reverse negative perceptions.

Recognizing and addressing predictive warning signs can help physicians confront job insecurity with confidence. By staying informed and proactive, you can safeguard your professional future and ensure a smoother transition to new opportunities, should the need arise.

Remember, your career is a journey, and each challenge presents an opportunity for growth and advancement. Job loss resembles the opening of a window: it may initially feel like an unwelcome draft, but it also provides fresh air and new perspectives, leading to growth and transformation.

Use AI to Say Goodbye to Endless Job Searches

*Use artificial intelligence to help you
unlock employment opportunities.*

LANDING YOUR DREAM JOB DOESN'T have to be a tedious, never-ending process. With ChatGPT — a highly popular artificial intelligence (AI) chatbot that can generate human-like text and computer code in response to user prompts — you can supercharge your job search and possibly secure a position more quickly than by searching for jobs traditionally. Below, I explore powerful ChatGPT prompts that can enhance your resume, streamline your job applications, and prepare you for interviews. First, some background.

How It Works

OpenAI, an AI research company, created ChatGPT and released it in November 2022. ChatGPT uses a language model called the Generative Pre-trained Transformer (GPT) to process and analyze large amounts of data to generate responses. The model predicts the next word in a sequence based on the text on which it was trained. ChatGPT is trained using reinforcement learning, which means it receives feedback from humans to improve its responses. The basic software is free to download, and there are upgrades you can pay for.

ChatGPT can:

- Understand human language as it's spoken and written.
- Answer questions.
- Compose written content, such as articles, social media posts, emails, and code.
- Recommend correct grammar and syntax.
- Build resumes and write cover letters.
- Brainstorm, prompt you with questions, and help you find inspiration.

ChatGPT is similar to the automated chat services found on customer service websites. It can also be used in job applications to help with resumes, cover letters, and more.

Cracking Your Dream Job

To start, you can use ChatGPT to review job descriptions. Simply copy and paste the description of the job you're targeting and ask the tool to highlight the five most important responsibilities. This allows you to focus on the key aspects of the role and tailor your application to meet the employer's expectations effectively.

Networking is a crucial part of any job search. ChatGPT can help you create a customized connection message, for example, on LinkedIn. You might ask it to draft a message that introduces you to a professional at a company you're interested in, discussing your interest in a specific position and how your background aligns with the role. This personalized approach ensures your messages stand out in a competitive environment.

Refining your resume bullet points is another way to set yourself apart. By pasting a bullet point from your resume into ChatGPT and asking it to rewrite the text using compelling language and measurable metrics, you can significantly improve your resume's impact. Additionally, you can have ChatGPT review your skills against a job description to determine alignment and identify mismatches, providing actionable insights to refine your application materials.

When updating your resume for a specific role, ChatGPT can help focus on relevant skills and experiences. By providing both the job description and your current resume, the tool can craft a version that aligns perfectly with the employer's needs. Furthermore, it can assist in writing a personalized cover letter tailored to the job description and your qualifications, showcasing your enthusiasm and relevance.

Preparation for interviews is another area where ChatGPT excels. You can request a list of interview questions based on the job description or even simulate a technical mock interview. For example, you can ask ChatGPT to conduct a mock interview for a specific role by posing technical questions related to the field, enabling you to gauge your expertise and refine your answers. The tool can also help you craft a polished introduction for interviews, ensuring you make a strong first impression.

Addressing the Concerns Around AI in Job Searches

The integration of AI tools like ChatGPT into job search strategies has sparked debate, with critics voicing legitimate concerns about its implications. One critique is that relying on AI without applying critical reasoning could lead to generic outcomes, making applicants blend into the crowd.

To counteract this, job seekers must engage with AI as partners, not as substitutes. By issuing tailored and thought-provoking prompts, such as asking ChatGPT to analyze whether resumes or cover letters show signs of AI involvement and suggesting improvements, users can refine their submissions for authenticity and uniqueness.

Some skeptics dismiss these tools altogether, questioning whether AI-driven methodologies alone can secure a job. The truth is that ChatGPT cannot replace the effort required to deeply understand an organization, align with its values, and connect personally with hiring teams. While AI can help with presentation and preparation, a successful job search still demands human effort, homework, and genuine connections with recruiters and search committees. No tool can replace the understanding of the human needs behind the hiring process.

Another valid point often raised is that AI's contribution often ends at securing interviews. During the actual interview, physicians must rely on their knowledge, interpersonal skills, and confidence to make an impression. AI may prepare job seekers by providing mock interviews or crafting practice responses, but the interview itself is a personal engagement where only the individual's authenticity and preparation matter.

The human connection is often cited as a missing element in AI-driven strategies — not only in job searches but in the practice of medicine in general. Contact with people remains as timeless and effective as an approach to finding a job as it is to medical practice.

AI should not overshadow this fundamental principle. Nurturing professional relationships and demonstrating genuine interest require a personal touch that AI cannot replicate.

Ethical concerns have also surfaced regarding the use of AI in crafting application materials. Some argue that presenting AI-enhanced resumes and cover letters might be deceptive. However, using AI to help express one's strengths and experiences is not inherently unethical. What matters is honesty — ensuring that the final output reflects your real capabilities and achievements.

Moreover, while AI might prove particularly useful in enterprise-level hiring processes, its impact can vary in smaller healthcare organizations or private entities where hiring decisions are less standardized. In these settings, direct interaction and technical evaluations often carry more weight than polished application materials. Recognizing these subtleties allows you to adapt their approach and use AI where it has the most value.

Also, keep in mind that, ironically, AI is being used to detect its own usage. For example, college instructors use their own brand of AI to detect students' use of AI in writing. This contradiction — AI as both enabler and watchdog — signals the need for a more complete understanding of its role.

Rather than viewing AI as a shortcut or a deception, we should recognize it as a collaborative assistant that complements, rather than competes with, human ingenuity. By having this perspective, we can shift the focus from whether AI was used to how effectively it enhances authenticity, productivity, and value in professional contexts.

Ultimately, AI like ChatGPT should not replace old-fashioned networking or the hard work of building genuine connections — at work or in the exam room. Instead, it should act as a catalyst that empowers job seekers to present themselves effectively, articulate their strengths clearly, and prepare for opportunities with confidence. By balancing AI tools with traditional job search methods, physicians may be able to enhance their chances of success while maintaining the personal touch that makes their applications stand out.

Find Your "Fit" in the Organization

Physicians who attain a good job fit are more likely to be happy and productive.

PHYSICIANS SHOULD CONSIDER THE "GOODNESS of fit" between themselves and any organization they consider working for. In the field of statistics, goodness of fit describes how well a model correlates with actual observations or values.

Organizational psychologists borrowed the term to describe the compatibility of a person's temperament and skills with workplace requirements and environment. The interaction between workplace variables and physician characteristics significantly influences the effects of work. The ultimate consequence of a poor fit is disillusionment, pessimism, burnout, and depression.

Although no single set of job characteristics is good or bad for everyone, and although job requirements may change over time, many conditions are important, perhaps prerequisite, for a good fit between physicians and organizations and may diminish dissatisfaction and burnout. These include:

Type of Organization

Clinical clerkships in medical school may help physicians gauge the type of organization they might want to work for — large or small, profit versus nonprofit, hospitalist or outpatient, academic versus community, religious or nondenominational — by offering firsthand experience that highlights the importance of goodness of fit in aligning personal values and career goals with the organizational culture and work environment.

Reporting Relationships

The person a physician reports to may be the number one factor determining goodness of fit. As mentioned in essay 49, a disproportionate number of physicians lose their jobs when they have persistent conflicts with their bosses. Moreover, new bosses may be intent on replacing their direct reports with friends and former colleagues in a proverbial housecleaning.

Poor leadership qualities have negative effects on the personal well-being and job satisfaction of the physicians they lead — they burn them out over time. Physicians who report directly to non-physician administrators often experience personality clashes.

Communication
Joseph Grenny, co-author of the book *Crucial Conversations* and the *Physician Executive* article "Speak Up or Burn Out,"[1] observes that physicians who engage more consistently and effectively in conversations that strengthen their social support systems and give them a greater sense of efficacy are less likely to burn out. Crucial conversations also breed powerful organizations toward which physicians gravitate.

Career Development
Physicians often cite stalled careers and lack of opportunity for advancement as reasons for dissatisfaction. Although many physicians are content to practice continuously in the same specialty, a significant number seek career changes or plan to alter their practice patterns, creating a fundamental disconnect between what provides physicians with the most professional satisfaction and what others expect them to do.

Clear and Unambiguous Roles
Role conflict and role ambiguity are significant factors in work stress among employees. Dealing with ambiguity in the workplace is frustrating because ambiguity entails uncertainty, which causes leadership teams to become indecisive and unable to plan or make firm commitments. An entire organization suffering from inaction is counterproductive to physicians' work ethic.

Goal Alignment
Organizations and physicians need to align their goals to create safe and high-quality care at lower costs. Mutually rewarding goals lead not only to business success but also to personal satisfaction. Goals

that resonate with one's sense of purpose and meaning are likely to appeal to physicians, as are personal challenges and projects that lead to highly valued outcomes.

Rewards and Retention

Formalized physician retention programs are growing in popularity. Retention programs have been shown to be particularly effective in reducing separation, especially among early-career physicians. Common incentives are relocation assistance, income guarantee, signing and/or retention bonus, educational loan forgiveness, and malpractice insurance, including "tail" coverage.

Other "perks" may include an expense account, professional dues, journal subscriptions, CME expense reimbursement, research stipends, honoraria, and paid time off beyond vacation. If structured appropriately, rewards provide a competitive advantage in recruitment and retention and help create an esprit de corps among the medical staff.

Social Engagement

Collegial relationships are a major source of satisfaction for physicians. Although physicians relish clinical autonomy, they also appreciate a workplace where they can interact and network with peers, be recognized for good performance, and be included in management decisions. Safe and pleasant working conditions coupled with family-friendly policies help create job flexibility and work-life balance, which are important to job satisfaction.

Culture

Organizational culture encompasses values and behaviors that contribute to the unique social and psychological environment of a business. The culture of organizations may be evident through written and unwritten "rules of engagement," such as vision and mission statements, profit status, and spiritual affiliation (written), or a set of shared assumptions that guide behaviors (unwritten).

When physicians do not identify with the corporate culture, the result is a lack of trust, involvement, communication, and responsiveness to problem-solving. The inability or unwillingness to comply with cultural norms is a significant driver of physician turnover, more so than inadequate compensation and other sources of job dissatisfaction.

Conclusion

Few individuals are able to treat work solely as an impersonal activity. More than most professionals, physicians find it difficult to disengage from work to the point that many succumb to burnout and physical illness rather than walking away from a poor-fitting workplace. A careful assessment of the goodness of fit before accepting a job may result in job longevity and increased job satisfaction, as well as a more fulfilling and productive career.

Author Note: This essay is adapted with permission from Avoid Burnout by Finding Your 'Fit' in the Organization. *Physician Leadership Journal.* 2020;7(1):38–40. https://www.physicianleaders. org/articles/avoid-burnout-finding-your-fit-organization

REFERENCE

1. Grenny J. Speak Up or Burn Out. *Physician Executive.* 2006;32(6):24–28.

How to Prioritize Your Well-Being (Without Sacrificing Your Career)

It's more than permissible to take care of yourself — it's a prerequisite for attending to patients.

As PHYSICIANS, WE ARE OFTEN expected to embody resilience and selflessness, prioritizing the needs of our patients and careers above all else. While dedication is integral to our profession, the narrative that success requires sacrificing personal well-being is not only outdated but unsustainable.

The truth is, you deserve to thrive without compromising your health or happiness. By building intentional habits and shifting your mindset, you can achieve a fulfilling balance between professional success and personal wellness.

The Foundation for Well-Being

One of the most critical foundations for well-being is setting personal boundaries. As discussed in essay 46, begin by establishing non-negotiable rituals — small, daily practices that protect your energy and uphold discipline. Whether it's a morning walk, a meditation session, or a quiet cup of coffee before the day begins, these rituals create a sense of stability and focus amid the chaos of a demanding career.

Self-care, too, must become a top priority, scheduled as diligently as any critical meeting or patient appointment. Regular exercise, healthy eating, and restorative sleep boost your physical health and sharpens your mental clarity and overall productivity.

Mindset plays a pivotal role in sustaining both performance and wellness. Starting your day with a moment of stillness — through mindfulness, reflection, or journaling — helps anchor your thoughts and reduce stress, setting the tone for a more focused and centered day.

As mentioned repeatedly in this book, the ability to say "no" strategically is another essential skill (refer to essay 20 for a refresher). Each time you decline a task that doesn't align with your priorities, you are preserving time and energy for your most meaningful "yes."

Redefining productivity by focusing on impact rather than hours worked is equally transformative. Measuring success by the quality of your contributions rather than sheer effort allows you to maximize meaningful output without overextending yourself.

To maintain consistent energy and focus, optimize the structure of your day. A midday energy check — such as a brief walk or a few moments of deep breathing — prevents burnout and helps you recalibrate for the afternoon. Creating intentional bookends for your day, including morning intentions and evening reflections, provides both clarity and closure, helping you stay present and grounded.

Even your commute can serve as a mindset ritual, allowing you to prepare for peak performance or decompress after a demanding shift. Listen to soothing music, an informative podcast, or whatever feels right for the moment.

Understanding your natural energy rhythms is another key to optimizing performance. Take time to audit your peak periods of focus and energy, aligning your most challenging tasks with those times. Protecting deep work time by setting clear digital boundaries minimizes distractions and ensures that your attention remains on what matters most.

Managing Stress

Stress, an ever-present feature of medicine, can be managed through intentional practices. Breathwork mastery — a simple yet powerful tool described in many self-improvement books — enhances decision-making and helps you remain composed under pressure. Equally important is investing in a support system. Surround yourself with mentors, colleagues, and loved ones who can provide guidance and encouragement. These connections not only enrich your professional life but also serve as a vital source of strength during challenging times.

Ultimately, well-being drives success — not the reverse. To thrive as a physician, you must prioritize self-care and protect your core energy. When you integrate these strategies into your daily routine, you'll find that sustainable success becomes more than a goal — it becomes your reality. Success and well-being are not opposing forces; they are mutually reinforcing. You can achieve both with grace and longevity by creating a balanced, intentional approach to your personal and professional life.

Finding Strength in Simplicity

To skeptical physicians who might dismiss this advice as trite or overly simplistic, I'd say this: The simplicity of these strategies *is* their strength. Many of us, as physicians, are conditioned to seek complex solutions to complex problems, often overlooking the significant impact of foundational habits and mindset shifts. These strategies aren't meant to replace hard work or diminish the challenges of our profession — they're tools to help you work smarter and sustain yourself in a field where burnout is rampant.

If you find these ideas unconvincing, ask yourself: How many colleagues have I seen struggle under the weight of stress, exhaustion, and disillusionment? How many times have I, despite my best intentions, pushed my limits and ended up feeling depleted? These aren't rare occurrences — they're systemic issues. The strategies outlined here aren't magic fixes; they're practical, evidence-based practices that many high-performing professionals outside of medicine use successfully.

Skepticism is understandable, especially when wellness advice often feels generic or disconnected from the unique demands of our profession. But these approaches can be tailored to your reality.

For instance, a 10-minute morning stillness ritual isn't about finding time you don't have; it's about reclaiming time that might otherwise be consumed by checking emails or scrolling through your phone. Saying "no" strategically isn't about shirking responsibility — it's about ensuring you can give your best to what truly matters.

Conclusion

Finally, I'd remind skeptical colleagues that prioritizing well-being isn't just about individual benefit — it directly impacts patient care. A rested, focused, and emotionally resilient physician demonstrates better outcomes, communicates more effectively, and commands stronger therapeutic relationships. The small steps outlined here are not just about you; they're about the quality of care your patients deserve and the longevity of your career in medicine. Dismissing these strategies as simplistic may inadvertently perpetuate the culture of burnout that has plagued our profession for too long. Why not give simplicity a chance? The results might surprise you.

AFTERWORD

∞

To Practice or Not: Exploring Non-Clinical Careers

Non-clinical careers are well-suited for physicians drifting away from 1:1 patient care toward population health.

THIS BOOK WAS WRITTEN TO empower physicians to stay in practice, not to leave it. But let's face it. Every one of us has thought of exchanging our white coats for something different. More than a decade ago, a survey of over 6,000 physicians conducted by Mayo Clinic researchers showed that 2% of doctors were considering leaving the profession in the next two years to pursue a different career.[1] A 2023 Medscape survey indicated 26% are considering a non-clinical career path.[2]

The increased interest in alternative and non-clinical medical careers is fueled by a variety of factors, including burnout and a desire to work fewer and more stable hours. Other issues may include:

- Wanting to spend more time with family.
- Frustration with insurance companies.
- Age/retirement/leisure pursuits.
- Demanding work environments.
- Declining reimbursement for clinical care.
- Personal health problems or those of a family member.

Indentured Servants

Although most physicians subconsciously recognize the numerous and persistent challenges that impede their ability to reach their ultimate potential in medical practice, over time, as they persevere with the intense pressures, many physicians find themselves becoming what could be described as indentured servants to the medical-industrial complex: the intricate web of relationships among pharmaceutical companies, insurance providers, healthcare facilities, and government entities.

This dynamic, coupled with administrative manipulation of medical careers, largely stems from government efforts to exert control not only over healthcare systems but also over the medical profession itself. The consequences of this control, when combined with economic and operational challenges, leave many physicians questioning their career choices or seeking alternative paths.

Reinventing Yourself: The First Step to Transition

Physicians considering a non-clinical career often face the challenge of redefining their identity. The transition requires a mindset shift, moving from being defined by clinical skills and certifications to being evaluated based on outcomes and results. Frequently, the biggest hurdle is the physicians themselves. Rebranding yourself as a leader with transferable skills and showcasing your adaptability are critical steps to standing out in the non-clinical job market.

Debunking Myths About Career Transitions

When I transitioned from practice to full-time industry (health insurance), the constant refrain was:

Myth #1: "You're going over to the dark side."
Physicians exploring non-clinical roles often encounter skepticism from colleagues. However, opportunities in sectors like pharma, health policy, and leadership allow physicians to continue serving society by shaping patient care on a broader scale.

Staying true to your values and career goals is key. One of the greatest compliments I received was being called an "insider" by a physician who recognized that as a utilization reviewer, I was not there to deny care; rather, I fed him the appropriate medical jargon (criteria) to recite back to me in order to certify more time for his patient in the hospital.

Myth #2: "You're throwing away years of training and skills."
This misconception assumes that clinical practice is the only valid career path for a physician. In reality, the skills developed in clinical medicine — critical thinking, communication, and problem-solving — are invaluable in non-clinical roles. Transitioning doesn't mean

abandoning your expertise; it means applying it in new, impactful ways — and gaining more skills.

Myth #3: "You must go back to school to succeed."
Physicians often believe that obtaining additional degrees, like an MBA or MPH, is a prerequisite for non-clinical roles. While some careers require specific qualifications (*e.g.*, MD/JD), most do not. Instead, targeted skill development, such as public speaking or clinical trial management, can bridge gaps and prepare you for your next role.

Myth #4: "You must meet all job qualifications to apply."
Unlike clinical positions, where specific certifications are non-negotiable, non-clinical job descriptions are often aspirational. Physicians should focus on transferable skills and relevant experiences, even if they don't meet every qualification listed. You'll often see some qualifications listed as "desirable" rather than mandatory.

Myth #5: "Non-clinical roles pay less."
While some roles may initially offer lower salaries than clinical jobs, many non-clinical positions — especially in pharma, utilization management, and consulting — provide competitive compensation. Factoring in predictable schedules, fewer administrative burdens, and bonus and equity compensation often reveal a better hourly rate compared to clinical practice.

Diverse Career Opportunities
The spectrum of non-clinical roles available to physicians is vast. In the pharmaceutical and biotech sectors, physicians can influence drug development and regulatory strategies. Management consulting allows physicians to tackle healthcare challenges on a macro scale, leveraging their analytical and clinical expertise. Positions like chief medical officer (CMO) in health tech companies provide opportunities to drive innovation and align products with medical standards.

Other career paths include clinical operations, where you oversee healthcare delivery, and medical writing, which allows you to translate complex concepts into accessible language. Health policy roles and utilization management positions provide platforms for systemic change, improving healthcare efficiency and equity.

My favorite non-clinical job was in pharma, where I reviewed drug advertisements and promotional material for scientific accuracy and medical completeness (i.e., the truth). I even got to work with directors and actors on television commercials. As a psychiatrist, I was in the best position to advise them on how to portray a manic or depressive patient or how side effects like tardive dyskinesia should appear to viewers.

Broader Impacts and Macro-Level Change

Physicians can scale their impact beyond individual patient care by influencing policy, technology, and organizational culture, amplifying healthcare outcomes through leadership roles. By leveraging their expertise and passion, physicians can help design benefits and reshape healthcare systems to benefit countless patients. It was my interest in population health — not solely my struggle to overcome the trauma I described in the Prologue — that attracted me to the health insurance industry.

Overcoming Challenges and Finding Direction

Stepping off the well-trodden path of clinical practice can be daunting. Physicians accustomed to structured career trajectories may feel uncertain about where to begin. Reflecting on your passions and values can provide clarity. Aligning your core principles and core competencies with available options helps you chart a course.

Key Skills for Non-Clinical Success

Success in non-clinical roles demands a mix of traditional and new skills. Leadership, communication, and problem-solving remain essential. Physicians must also develop adaptive expertise and the ability to craft and execute innovative solutions to complex challenges. Targeted skill-building — whether through online courses or mentorship — can enhance your qualifications and confidence.

The Path Forward: Practical Steps

Transitioning to a non-clinical role starts with self-assessment. Identify your interests, transferable skills, and long-term goals. Networking is crucial; attend industry events, join online communities, and connect with professionals in your desired field. Tailor your resume and cover letter to highlight your achievements and flexibility.

Consider small, incremental steps, such as volunteering or part-time work, to gain experience and build confidence. Remember that rejection is part of the process (refer to essay 43) — persistence and a growth mindset will help you find the right fit.

Also, remember that the grass is not necessarily greener on the other side; it's just different. A non-clinical career works out best for physicians who feel pulled toward it, as opposed to wanting to escape the drudgery of practice.

Conclusion

Physicians exploring non-clinical careers have a wealth of opportunities to choose from, allowing them to make meaningful impacts beyond the bedside. By debunking common myths, embracing reinvention, and honing their skills, physicians can transition successfully into roles that align with their values and aspirations. Whether shaping policy, driving innovation, or contributing to health outcomes, the possibilities are endless for those willing to take the leap — and there are many fine resources to help you get started.

For example, *50 Nonclinical Careers for Physicians: Fulfilling, Meaningful, and Lucrative Alternatives to Direct Patient Care*, by Sylvie Stacy, MD, MPH, and *Inspiring Growth and Leadership in Medical Careers: Transform Healthcare as a Physician Leader*, by Peter Angood, MD, are well worth the read. Both books are published by the American Association for Physician Leadership (AAPL), the "home" for physician leaders and physicians seeking career transformations, whether clinical or non-clinical.

For physicians considering the plunge to business school, I heartily recommend my own book, *MD/MBA: Physicians on the New Frontier of Medical Management,* also published by AAPL.

Good luck!

REFERENCES

1. Shanafelt TD, Hasan O, Dyrbye LN, Satele D, Sloan J, West CP, *et al*. Changes in Burnout and Satisfaction with Work-Life Balance in Physicians and the General US Working Population Between 2011 and 2014. Mayo Clin Proc. 2015;90(120;1600–1613. https://www.mayoclinicproceedings.org/article/S0025-6196(15)00716-8/fulltext.

2. Winsborough H. When Practicing Medicine Becomes Unrewarding: Medscape Physicians and Nonclinical Careers Report 2023. Medscape. November 2023. https://www.medscape.com/slideshow/2023-nonclinical-careers-6016752

www.ingramcontent.com/pod-product-compliance
Lightning Source LLC
Chambersburg PA
CBHW061216220326
41599CB00025B/4660